KICKIN UP SOME

COWBOY FUN

130 ACTIVITIES FOR COWBOYS + COWGIRLS

Written by Monica Hay Cook   Illustrated by Jude Cook

Monjeu
PRESS

Tucson, Arizona

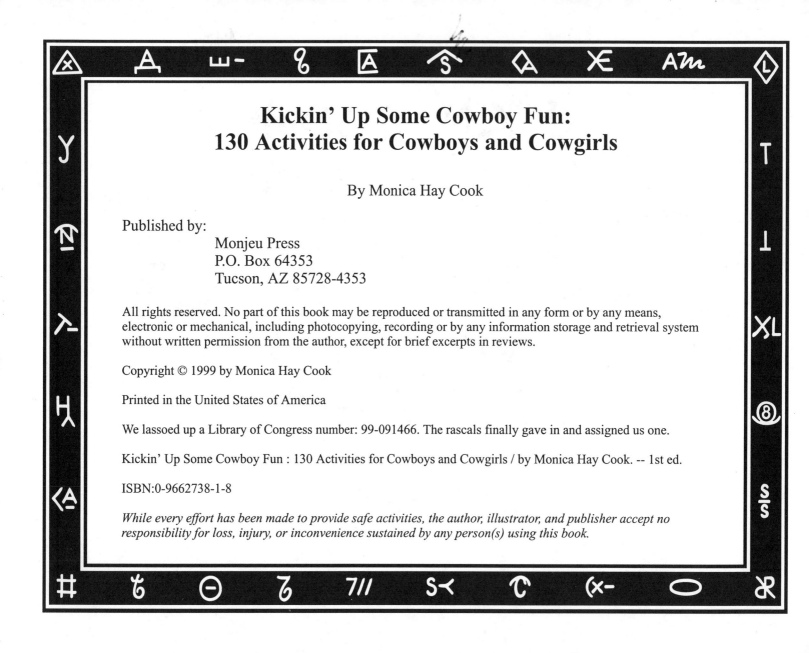

Kickin' Up Some Cowboy Fun:
130 Activities for Cowboys and Cowgirls

By Monica Hay Cook

Published by:

Monjeu Press
P.O. Box 64353
Tucson, AZ 85728-4353

Printed in the United States of America

We lassoed up a Library of Congress number: 99-091466. The rascals finally gave in and assigned us one.

Kickin' Up Some Cowboy Fun : 130 Activities for Cowboys and Cowgirls / by Monica Hay Cook. -- 1st ed.

ISBN:0-9662738-1-8

While every effort has been made to provide safe activities, the author, illustrator, and publisher accept no responsibility for loss, injury, or inconvenience sustained by any person(s) using this book.

Yipee-Yi-Yays!!!

Dedicated to two brave cowboys,
Jude and Chris.
They tasted all the grub from the recipes in this here book.
Several comments from these brave men worked their way into the pages of this book.

And for my busy little cowgirl, Erika.

--M.H.C.

Yahoos!!!

Here's to four root'n toot'n cowgirls.

Marie Cook
has graciously provided the silhouettes on the author/illustrator page. She is an accomplished artist. This fine lady is amazing with a pair of scissors. She can cut a person's profile in three minutes flat.

Dawn Dixon
has lived in the Southwest most of her life and knows the desert so well, she even knows the lizards by their first names. This gal read my book and gave me some great ideas for it. She's a mighty fine writer too.

Judy Dyl
has a degree in Creative Writing and worked as a technical editor. She gave excellent advice on the content and grammar in my book. She's got more words than a mail order catalog and uses them in her own writing as well.

Janice Mitich
grew up on ranches in Wyoming and Arizona, competed in rodeos, and now, among other things, writes and recites her cowboy poetry throughout the Southwest. She knows more about cattle than a coyote does about howlin' and took the time to read my book for accuracy.

A Note to Cowgirls

It's well known that cowboys dominated the scene in the old days, but there were some spunky and brave cowgirls too. It was uncommon for women to go on cattle drives, but some women did saddle their own horses, round up cattle, and worked on their family farms. Such behavior was looked down on, but it was this participation by women that set the stage for their independence and equal rights with men. While the text in this book often refers to the cowboy, it is this author's belief that cowgirls can do all these activities as well as cowboys. So, cowgirls and cowboys, I hope you have a walloping good time with these western activities.

Cowboy and Cowgirl Safety

It is this author's wish that the cowboys and cowgirls doing the activities in this book be safe. Activities that require cooking and adult supervision have been marked with the bull safety symbol. Cowboys and cowgirls, when doing an activity with the bull safety symbol, get your trail boss or parent to help you do this activity. Who knows, your trail boss may be hankerin' for some fun.

Cowboy and Cowgirl Appreciation

The inspiration for this writing came from a book about cowboys. It was the start to an entire year of reading and writing about cowboys and cowgirls of the Old West. The more I read, the greater appreciation I developed for the cowboys and cowgirls that took great risks everyday to protect the cattle they tended.

Most cowboys were young men in their teens and early twenties. Some had dreamt about becoming cowboys since their childhood. They were loyal to the rancher and the brand they worked for. Cowboys spent 10 to 14 hours a day in a saddle tending cattle, chasing strays, and mending fences. During the peak of the "cowboy era," about 1864 to the late 1880's, cowboys rounded up cattle and moved them to markets.

There was an unwritten code of honor in the West, which most cowboys understood and held to, but it was also a time of rugged desperation. The new frontier was not without some outlaws. But the number of bad guys and shoot-outs have been exaggerated by western movies, magazines, and books. Most cowboys never met any bank or stagecoach robbers, but they probably encountered cattle thieves.

Hope you enjoy learning about the cowboy of old and his way of life. Then kick up your heels and get set to have a mighty fun time doing the cowboy activities. Yipee-Yi-Yay!

Cowboy History

Before trail drives, chuck wagons, and roundups, cow herders traveled alone or in small groups rounding up their herds for branding and driving to market. A lone cowboy heading out on a trail took enough provisions to last him several days. On his saddle horn, he probably hung a bag of flour or cornmeal, corn bread, biscuits, some beef jerky, and a little salt or sugar. Often he ran out of supplies and had to stop at other ranches for food. Very little was hung on the saddle because things hanging there interfered with working cattle. At the most, a canteen, a riffle for protection against wild animals, and rope were tied to the front strings on the saddle. A cowboy's bedroll, slicker, and other personal items would be tied behind the cantle on the back skirt of the saddle, using the strings in back. A lone cowboy going a great distance would probably load food on a pack mule or horse.

Beginning around 1866, there was a great demand for Texas beef in the East and in Europe. About this time, Texans began calling themselves "cowboys." They spent months driving herds of cattle north to meet up with the railroads in Kansas and Missouri. Over the years, thousands of cowboys drove millions of cattle to markets on trails such as the Old Chisholm Trail and the Great Western Trail.

Homesteaders learned about the vast tracts of land available in the West, and they started moving there to farm and raise sheep. Easterners and Europeans heard about the money to be made raising cattle. Financiers poured money into the Great Plains. They bought ranches and combined them to become cattle barons. The ranchers needed many cowboys to tend to the cattle and manage their ranches. Cowboys became very important in shaping western history.

The Cowboy Code of Honor

In the old days, most cowboys were hard working fellows that lived by a code of honor. An honorable cowboy:

- ▶ always kept his word.
- ▶ acted on promises made with a handshake.
- ▶ didn't mess with someone else's horse.
- ▶ never cut in front of another rider.
- ▶ didn't crowd from behind either.
- ▶ never borrowed a horse without asking first.
- ▶ always closed gates behind himself.
- ▶ always put away his horse before he put away his dinner.

Create a Code of Honor

Translate these statements into ones that are relevant to you. For example, "A cowboy never borrowed a horse without asking first," could translate into "I never take someone else's stuff without asking first." Think of some other ways you can relate the cowboy code of honor to your life.

A Cowboy's Neckerchief

Cowboys wore neckerchiefs. "Neckerchief" is another name for the bandanna a cowboy wore around his neck. In windy weather, a cowboy pulled it over his nose and mouth to keep out blowing dust. In winter, he wore it under his eyes to cut the glare of snow. During cold winds, a cowboy tied it over his Stetson and under his chin to warm his ears and to keep his hat from blowing away. A neckerchief could be used as a wash cloth, a towel, a bandage for cuts, a sling for broken bones, and a hot pad during branding time. Cowboys usually wore dull red or tan neckerchiefs.

Make a Cowboy Neckerchief

Take a piece of red or tan cotton, cut the cloth 20 inches by 20 inches. Fold the cloth diagonally bringing the opposite corners together. Tie the cloth loosely in a knot around your neck. The triangular part in the front can be pulled over your nose and mouth. This will help protect your face from sleet and wind and dust. It could come in mighty handy when you do your chores.

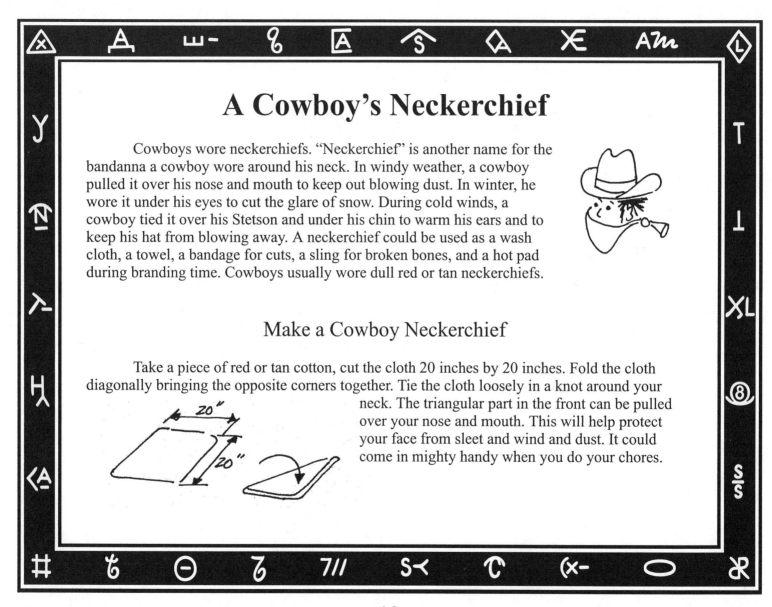

A Cowboy's Call to Dinner

Ding! Ding! Ding! "Chow! Come and git it" That's how a cook in the Old West announced meals. From his chuck wagon, he hung a triangular piece of iron, called an angle iron. When he struck it with a piece of metal, it rang loudly, alerting the cowboys to come and get their chow.

Make a Dinner Bell

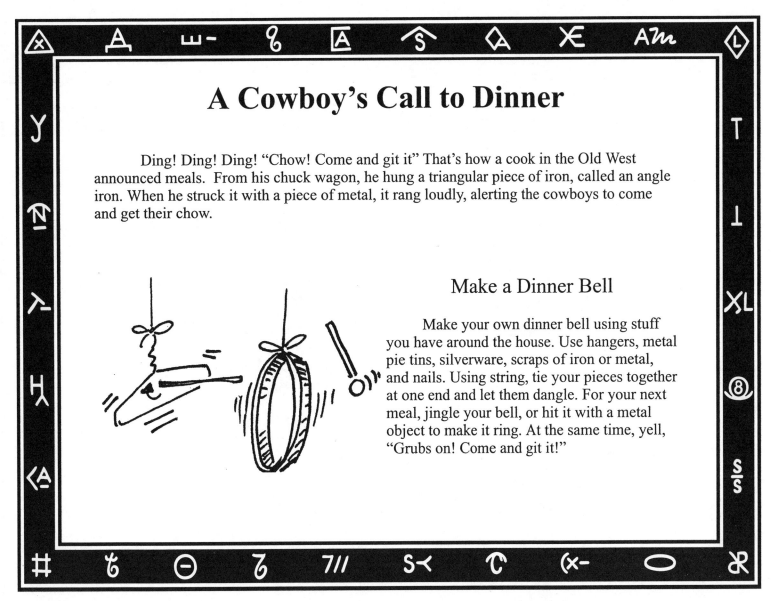

Make your own dinner bell using stuff you have around the house. Use hangers, metal pie tins, silverware, scraps of iron or metal, and nails. Using string, tie your pieces together at one end and let them dangle. For your next meal, jingle your bell, or hit it with a metal object to make it ring. At the same time, yell, "Grubs on! Come and git it!"

Not Beans Again!

Beans were the most common food around cow camps. The cow hands grew weary of them. They even made up other names for them, like "prairie whistles" and "Pecos strawberries." They had sayings about beans too, such as, "Oh, it's bacon and beans 'most everyday, I'd as soon be eatin' prairie hay." Pinto beans were the standard fair. Here's a recipe to try:

2 cups pinto beans
1 ½ quarts water
1 cup salt pork
1 tablespoon ground ginger
Salt
Pepper
Garlic

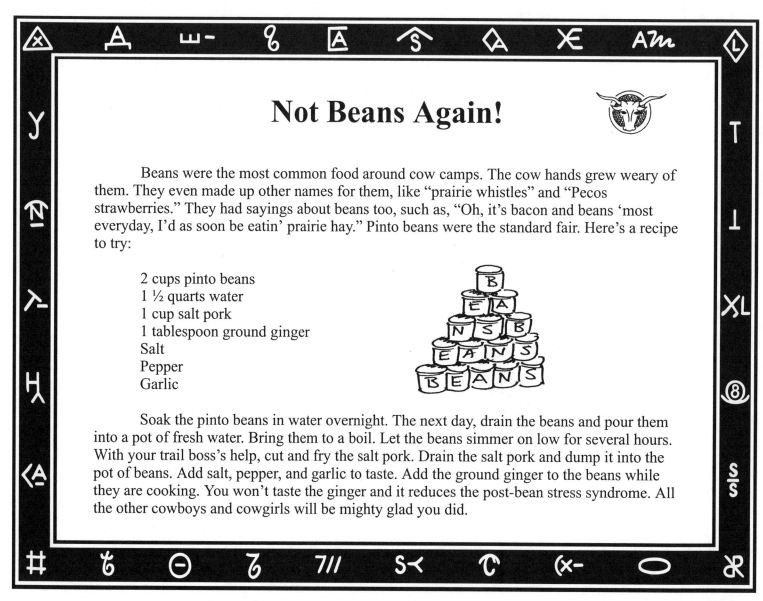

Soak the pinto beans in water overnight. The next day, drain the beans and pour them into a pot of fresh water. Bring them to a boil. Let the beans simmer on low for several hours. With your trail boss's help, cut and fry the salt pork. Drain the salt pork and dump it into the pot of beans. Add salt, pepper, and garlic to taste. Add the ground ginger to the beans while they are cooking. You won't taste the ginger and it reduces the post-bean stress syndrome. All the other cowboys and cowgirls will be mighty glad you did.

Troubles on the Trail

After the Civil War, there was a great demand for cattle in the growing new cities in the northern and eastern parts of the country. Cowboys were employed to drive longhorn cattle from the South to meet up with the railroads that would take the cattle to markets. The trail drive was headed up by the trail boss. He rode ahead and scouted out the best route, but even so the cowboys encountered many troubles while on a trail drive, such as wild animals, cattle rustlers, quicksand, and storms that made the cattle and horses nervous. The animals got "antsy" when a storm came in or the wind blew, because they couldn't smell or hear as well. A flash of lightning, or even a rustling leaf, could cause a stampede. On a windy day, high waves at a river crossing could be dangerous or keep the cattle from swimming across.

Take Your Cattle on the Trail

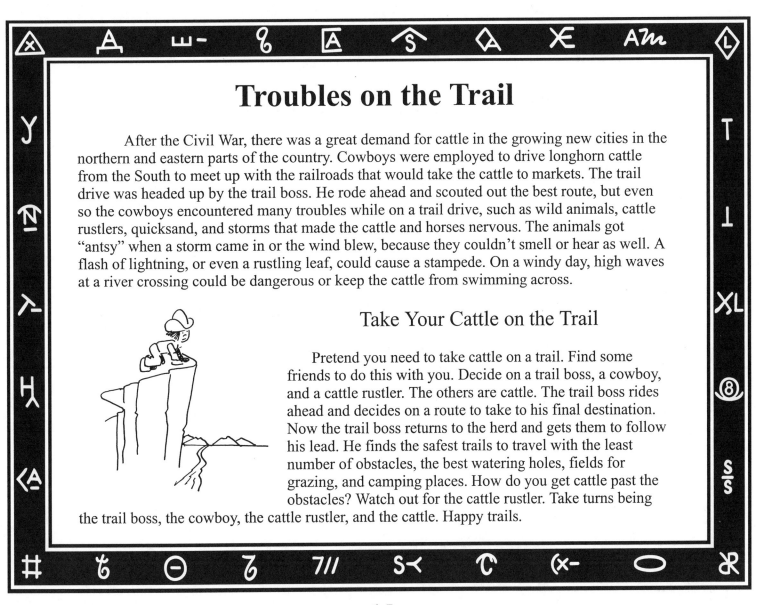

Pretend you need to take cattle on a trail. Find some friends to do this with you. Decide on a trail boss, a cowboy, and a cattle rustler. The others are cattle. The trail boss rides ahead and decides on a route to take to his final destination. Now the trail boss returns to the herd and gets them to follow his lead. He finds the safest trails to travel with the least number of obstacles, the best watering holes, fields for grazing, and camping places. How do you get cattle past the obstacles? Watch out for the cattle rustler. Take turns being the trail boss, the cowboy, the cattle rustler, and the cattle. Happy trails.

Cowboys Used a Blind Post Office

In the old days, outlaws or rustlers left notes to each other in crevices in rocks or tree trunks. Sheep herders and cowboys also left notes, some of them in tin cans buried under a pile of rocks called a sheep herder's monument. Those following the trail at a later time would uncover the notes.

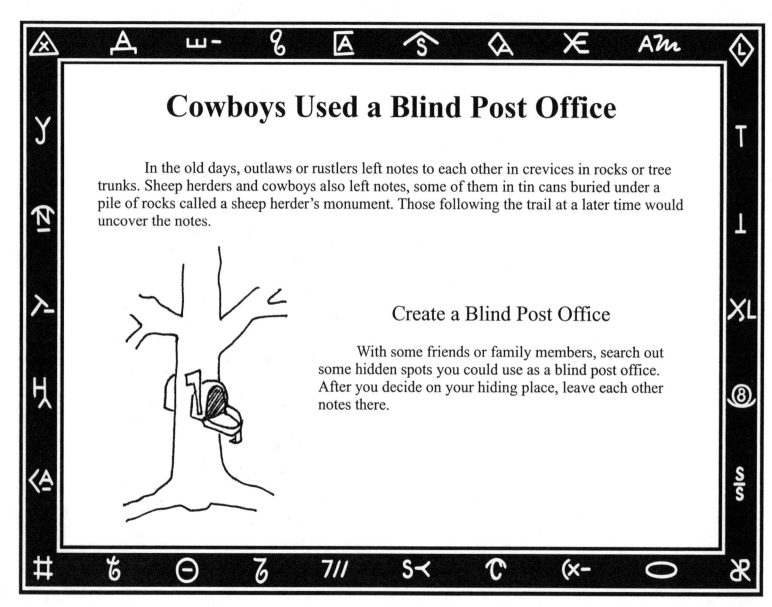

Create a Blind Post Office

With some friends or family members, search out some hidden spots you could use as a blind post office. After you decide on your hiding place, leave each other notes there.

Bobwire is Here to Stay

Barbed wire is formed from strands of wire twisted together with spikes or barbs fastened into the strands to keep critters in or out of a pasture. Cowboys called barbed wire "bobwire." Although the rights to bobwire were taken out several years earlier, Joseph F. Glidden is called the "father of bobwire." He took out a patent on bobwire in 1873.

Homesteaders moving to the West fenced the land they claimed with bobwire. It was much more reasonably priced than wood fencing. Bobwire caught on and spread quickly throughout the West. Ranchers hated barbed wire. They wanted to keep the ranges open, but they were eventually forced to fence too. Cattle would not go near the sharp spikes on bobwire if they could help it, but the fences still had to be maintained. This was called "ridin' fence."

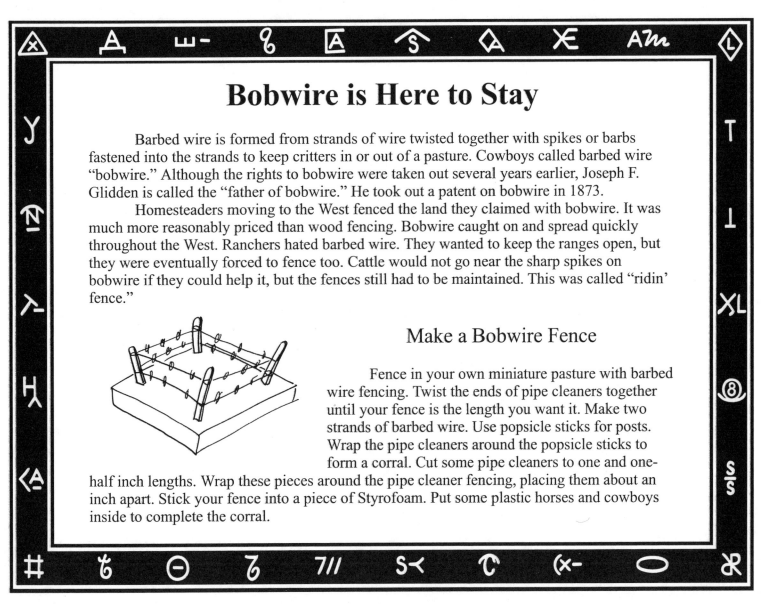

Make a Bobwire Fence

Fence in your own miniature pasture with barbed wire fencing. Twist the ends of pipe cleaners together until your fence is the length you want it. Make two strands of barbed wire. Use popsicle sticks for posts. Wrap the pipe cleaners around the popsicle sticks to form a corral. Cut some pipe cleaners to one and one-half inch lengths. Wrap these pieces around the pipe cleaner fencing, placing them about an inch apart. Stick your fence into a piece of Styrofoam. Put some plastic horses and cowboys inside to complete the corral.

Thirsty Cowboys

Cowboys got mighty thirsty on those hot dusty days when they rode the range or while on a trail drive. They had to be careful not to get dehydrated from lack of drinking water. They couldn't always count on water being available. In the summer, water holes dried up and streams could not be counted on to run, so the cowboys carried water with them. They used canteens, metal bottles, covered with wet felt or burlap and filled with water. The wet material helped keep the water inside cool. A cowboy tied it to the saddle strings when he rode the range.

Make a Canteen

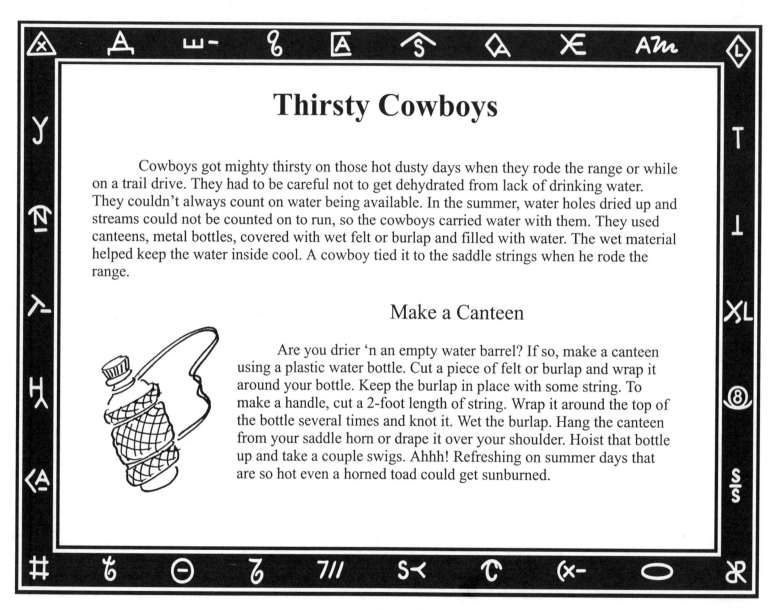

Are you drier 'n an empty water barrel? If so, make a canteen using a plastic water bottle. Cut a piece of felt or burlap and wrap it around your bottle. Keep the burlap in place with some string. To make a handle, cut a 2-foot length of string. Wrap it around the top of the bottle several times and knot it. Wet the burlap. Hang the canteen from your saddle horn or drape it over your shoulder. Hoist that bottle up and take a couple swigs. Ahhh! Refreshing on summer days that are so hot even a horned toad could get sunburned.

The Chuck Wagon

Charles Goodnight is credited with making the first chuck wagon in 1866. It was a wooden cupboard bolted to the back of an army wagon. Chuck wagons were also made using four-wheeled farm wagons and setting a chuck box on the back. This chuck box had shelves and drawers to carry cooking supplies and food. The back of the chuck wagon folded down to make a table for the cook to use. Chuck wagons were covered with canvas. All the drovers' bedrolls were thrown in the back. It also carried extra bedding and clothes. The chuck wagon was so helpful to the cowboy, that it became a commercially manufactured item. Chuck wagons sold for $75 to $100.

Make a Chuck Wagon

Put some boxes in a wagon for storage and put a sheet over it. Get ready to go on a cattle drive. Gather some cooking supplies, a "wreck pan" for your dirty dishes, bedding, and extra clothes. Don't forget some grub! Make your meal there in the chuck box. When finished, pull out the wreck pan and wash the dishes. Now get out your bedroll and git yourself some shut-eye.

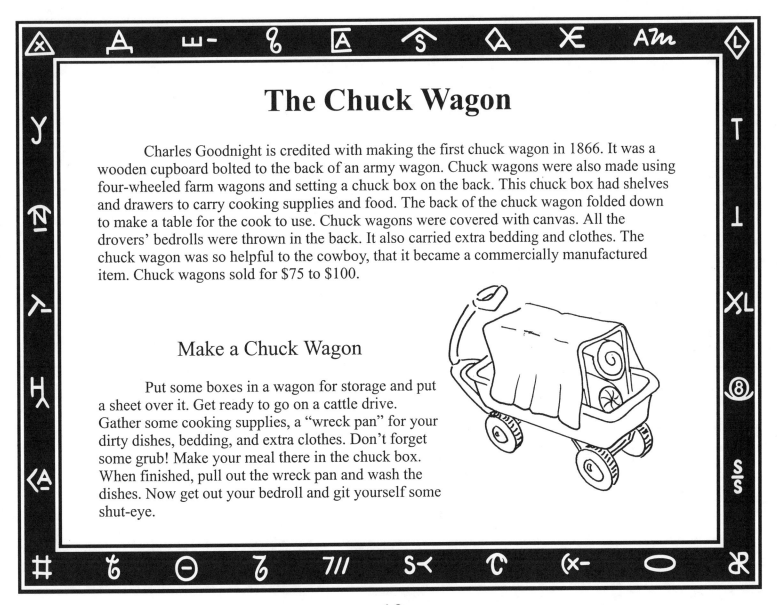

19

Brand Your Cattle

A brand is a permanent mark of ownership on the skin or hide of an animal. Each ranch had its own identifying brand. Brands were designed with some simple rules in mind. Brands read from left to right, top to bottom, and from the outside to the inside. The cowboys used figures in many of the brands they designed. A short line was called a bar, a longer line a rail. A square in a brand was usually called a box. A circle often had a letter in it and would be read from the outside to the inside, for example, circle C. A flattened circle was a goose egg. A flattened circle with a line through it became a buckle. An H with a half circle under it was called rocking H. Cowboys used moons, diamonds, and benches too.

Create Your Own Brand

With you trail boss's help, cut a large potato in half. Using a potato peeler, carve your design into one of the halves. When finished, dip the design into a shallow bowl of tempera paint and stamp your items.

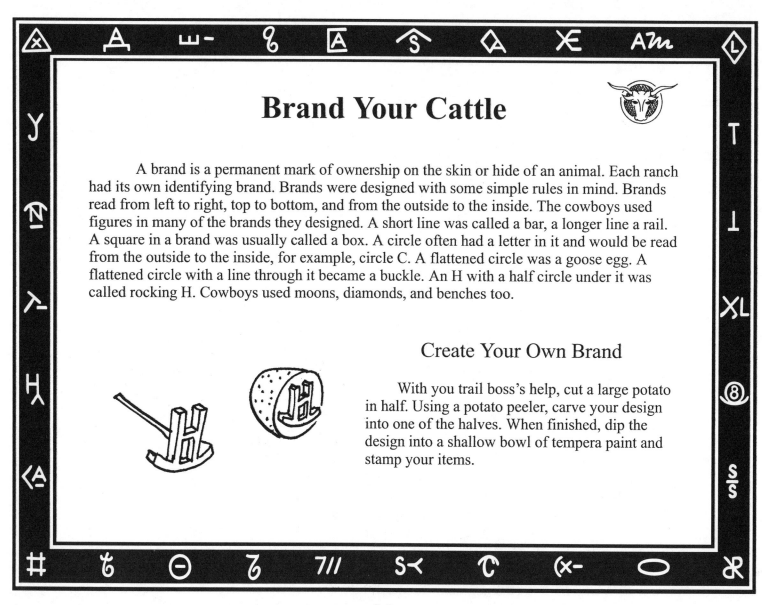

Mavericks

Maverick is another word for an orphaned or unmarked animal. Long-horned cattle, descended from cattle brought by the Spaniards, roamed freely. After Texas became a Republic, the law said a cowboy could catch wild longhorns, brand them, and add them to his herd. Some new settlers got their start this way. But even so, it was no easy task catching the wild long-horned cattle. They hid during the day among the chaparral, a Spanish word for dense, thorny brush or trees that grow in the Southwest. They could smell humans coming. Cowboys rode the range looking for the hidden cattle. They used decoy cattle to lure the wild ones out. Sometimes they worked at night catching cattle near their water holes.

Catch Some Mavericks

Gather some friends. Decide who will become pretend cattle and hide among the trees. Several of you are cowboys, cowgirls, and tame decoy cattle. The cowboys and cowgirls move among the trees and round up the cattle. Use decoy cattle to help lure them out. When a cattle is touched, it has to follow the cowboy. Take turns being the cowboys and cowgirls and the cattle.

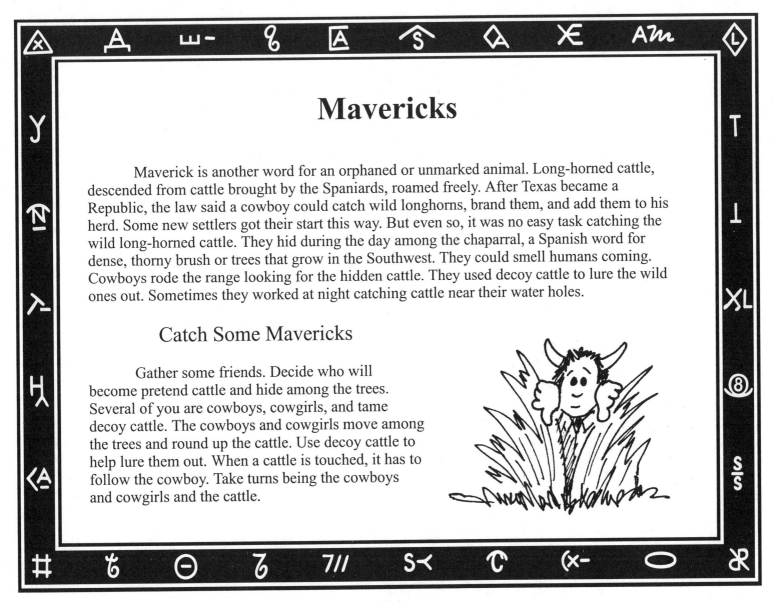

Cowboy Jingle-Bobs

Jingle-bobs or danglers are pear shaped ornaments made from metal. At the back of the heel band on a spur is a shank and at the end of the shank, there's a wheel. The wheel is called a rowel. It is held in place by a pin. This is where the jingle-bob dangles and jingles when a cowboy walks. Rumor has it, if a cowboy wanted to attract attention, he unfastened one of the chains on a boot. The wheel and the jingle-bob would jangle along the ground.

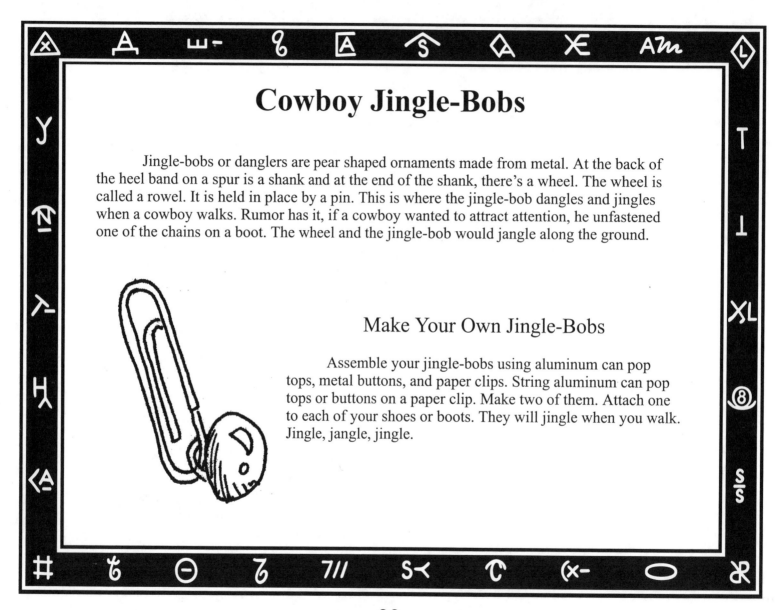

Make Your Own Jingle-Bobs

Assemble your jingle-bobs using aluminum can pop tops, metal buttons, and paper clips. String aluminum can pop tops or buttons on a paper clip. Make two of them. Attach one to each of your shoes or boots. They will jingle when you walk. Jingle, jangle, jingle.

Riding Sign

Frequently, cowboys were on the lookout for lost horses or cattle, but sometimes they had to track outlaws. "Riding sign" meant following the trail of an animal or person. The term "fresh sign" was used for a hot trail and "old sign" for an old trail. A good tracker watched for footprints and specific markings made by shoes or boots, such as a worn boot heel. Trackers looked for a broken horseshoe, chips off an animal's hoof, broken sticks, breaks in thickets, trampled grass, clues in the dirt, such as a rock that was out of place, or a deserted campfire. A good tracker could tell if an animal was walking, trotting, or galloping by the hoofprints left behind. Cowboys even watched for the tracks wild animals made, because they scampered away from a disturbance. A person being pursued might try backtracking or wading in and out on the same side of a stream. A good tracker used his brain to figure out where the person was going and tried to head him off.

Can You Read Signs?

With your friends, take turns leaving some clues and having others follow the signs to discover who or what is hidden. How good a tracker are you? Could you track bugs in a blizzard? Careful you don't smell out the wrong steer's butt.

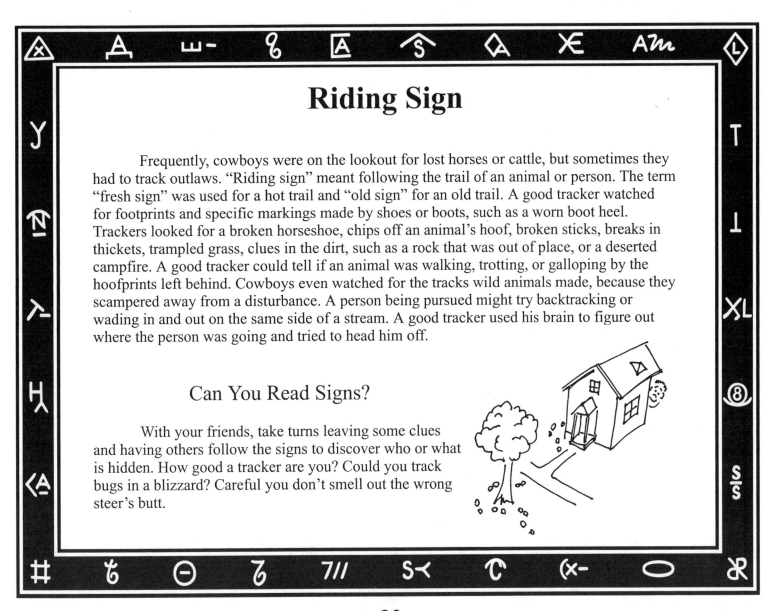

Measuring Horses

A hand is four and a half inches. Cowboys use this measurement to tell the height of their horses. The cowboy begins by using his hand flat against his horse at the ground near one of the hooves. He moves up one hand at a time until he reaches the horse's shoulder. The horse is said to be so many hands high.

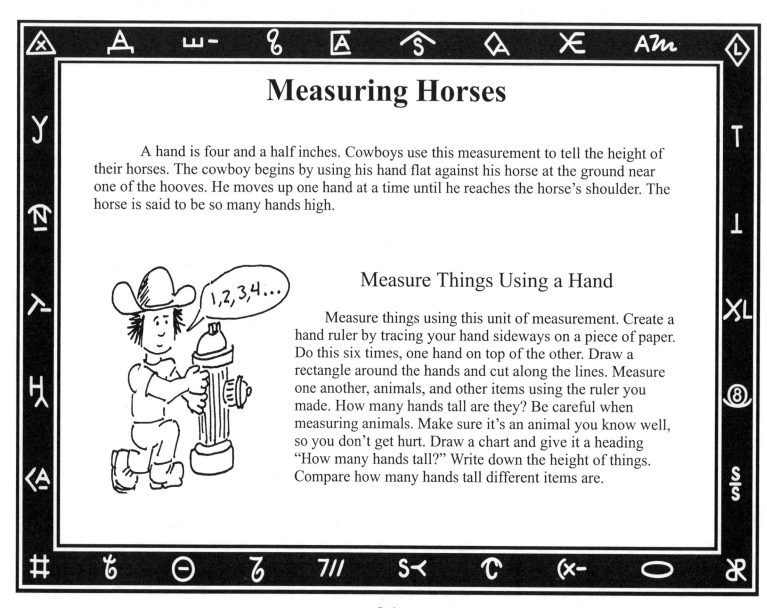

Measure Things Using a Hand

Measure things using this unit of measurement. Create a hand ruler by tracing your hand sideways on a piece of paper. Do this six times, one hand on top of the other. Draw a rectangle around the hands and cut along the lines. Measure one another, animals, and other items using the ruler you made. How many hands tall are they? Be careful when measuring animals. Make sure it's an animal you know well, so you don't get hurt. Draw a chart and give it a heading "How many hands tall?" Write down the height of things. Compare how many hands tall different items are.

Cowboys Fight Boredom

Have you ever played "Know Your Cans"? The cowboys did during the long winters when they had little to do. Cowboys who could read kept a book, often a Bible, to read and re-read. They read the newspaper pages pasted to the walls of their cabins to keep the wind from blowing in. If they ran out of other things to read, they would study the labels on canned foods and memorize them. The game was to recite the labels exactly as they were printed on cans, including punctuation.

Play the Game "Know Your Cans"

With some cowboy and cowgirl friends, pull out some cans to study and take turns memorizing the writing on the cans. Then recite the label from memory. Don't forget those commas and periods!

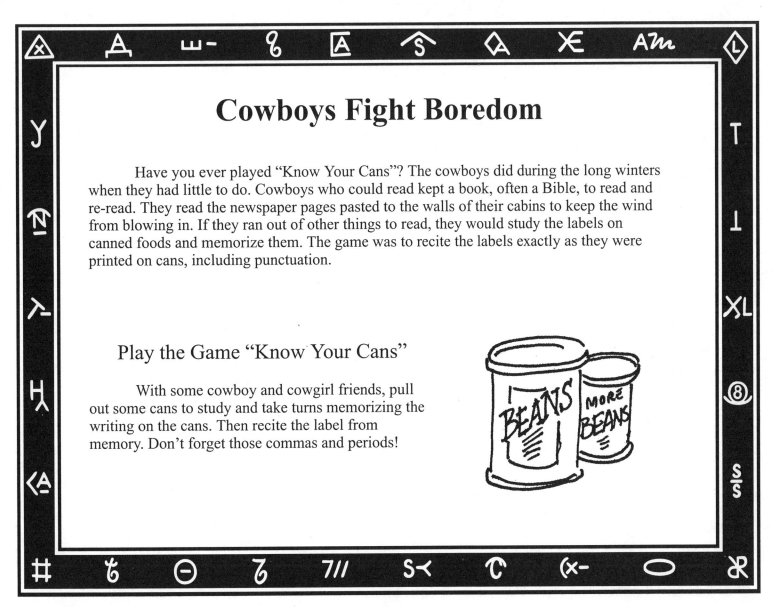

Cowboys Tie Knots

The cowboys knew how to intertwine rope or cord and make various kinds of knots. They used knots to tie up horses, cattle, gear, and for securing loads on pack saddles. Cowboys practiced knots in their spare time. Some cowboys knew how to make harder knots than others did and kept these methods a secret. Then they charged others fifty to seventy-five cents to tie those knots for them.

Tie Some Knots

Pull out some cord to practice making knots. How many different kinds of knots do you know? When you master them, have fun teaching the knots to your friends.

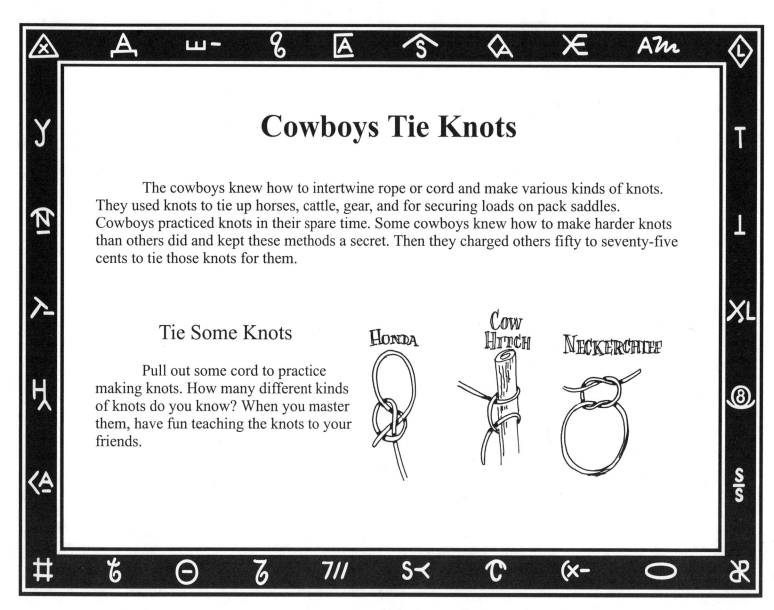

HONDA

COW HITCH

NECKERCHIEF

A Cowboy's Handle

A "handle" can be a person's full name or a nickname. In the old days, it was considered rude to ask a stranger his name or ask about his background, so the cowboys would ask someone what his handle was. A nickname usually came from something the person had done, the place where he was from or gained his reputation, or some personal characteristic, for example, "Wild James, Long Joe or Texas Bill." Some cowboys used handles, because they were hiding out from the law.

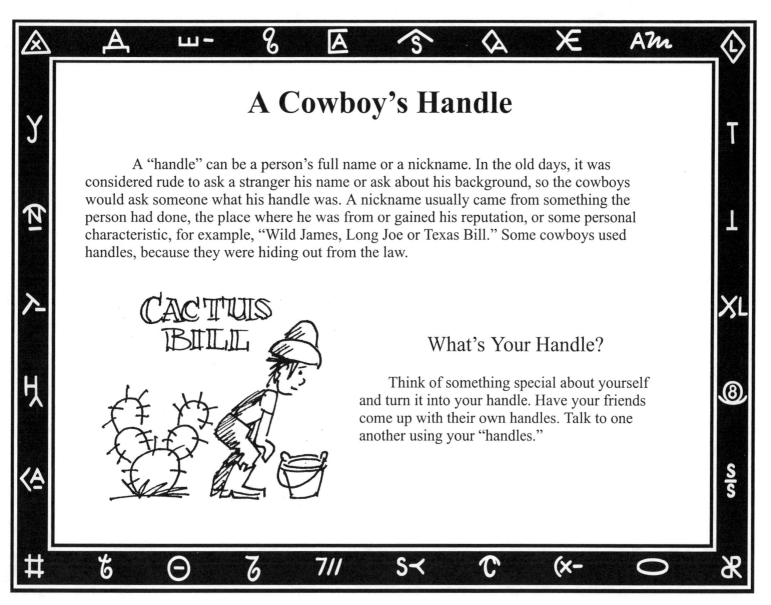

What's Your Handle?

Think of something special about yourself and turn it into your handle. Have your friends come up with their own handles. Talk to one another using your "handles."

Rattlers Lurk About

Whoa! Don't sit there. A cowboy always checks the ground before sitting. When he sleeps on the ground, he loops a horsehair rope around himself, because he thinks the rattlers won't cross the hairs. Upon wakening, he lies still to make sure no rattlers crawled under his blanket or on his chest.

Watch Out for Rattlers

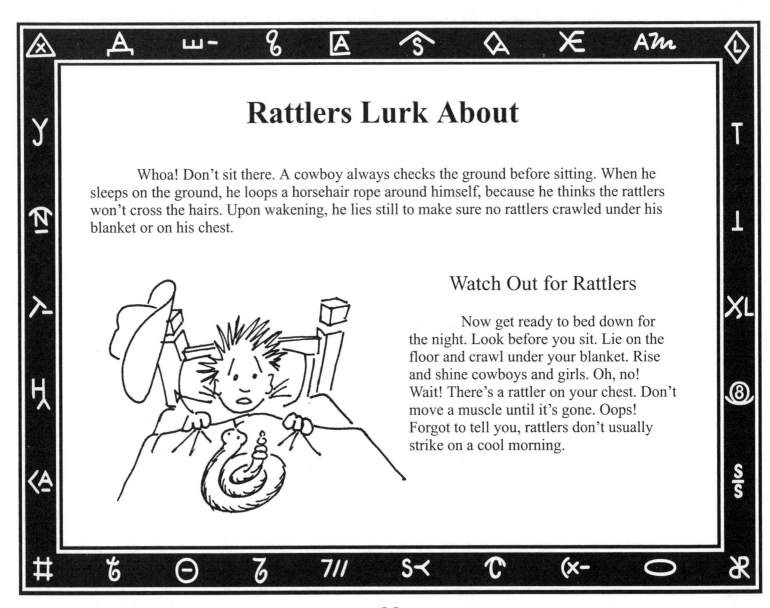

Now get ready to bed down for the night. Look before you sit. Lie on the floor and crawl under your blanket. Rise and shine cowboys and girls. Oh, no! Wait! There's a rattler on your chest. Don't move a muscle until it's gone. Oops! Forgot to tell you, rattlers don't usually strike on a cool morning.

The Cookie Calls

It's time to wake up like the cowboys. One old-time cowboy wake-up call went like this:

> Bacon in the pan.
> Coffee in the pot.
> Get up an' get it!
> Eat it while it's hot.

Sometimes the cook, who was nicknamed Cookie, wasn't in a good mood. Those days he yelled something like this, "Come and get it, or I'll throw it in the creek."

Think of Some Wake-Up Calls

Gather some friends together for a sleepover. Before you go to sleep, think up some wake-up calls. In the morning, take turns calling out your wake-up calls.

"BACON IN THE PAN COFFEE IN THE POT"

GET UP AN' GET IT!
EAT IT WHILE IT'S HOT!

The Cowboy's Boots

Early boots were square-toed and could be worn on either foot. A cowboy molded them to his feet by wearing them into a creek and then walking with them until they fit. This practice was certain to make that cowboy's feet mighty sore, although he probably didn't complain.

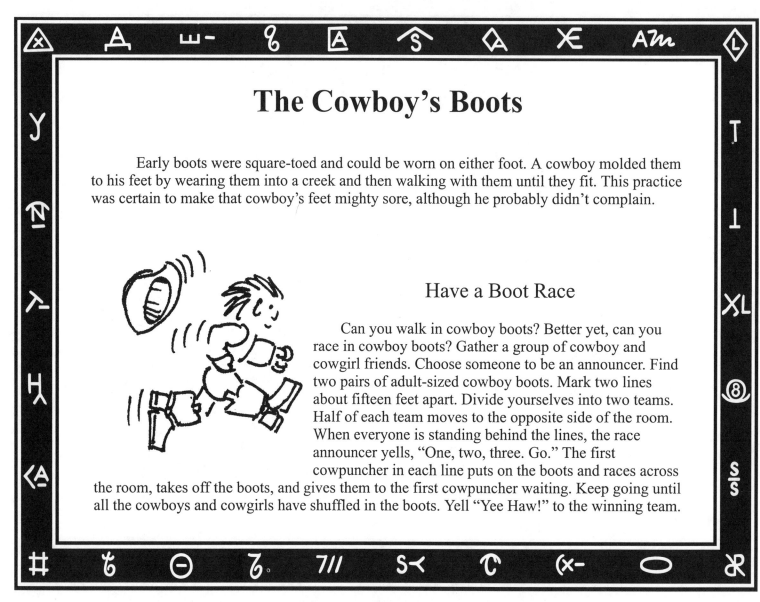

Have a Boot Race

Can you walk in cowboy boots? Better yet, can you race in cowboy boots? Gather a group of cowboy and cowgirl friends. Choose someone to be an announcer. Find two pairs of adult-sized cowboy boots. Mark two lines about fifteen feet apart. Divide yourselves into two teams. Half of each team moves to the opposite side of the room. When everyone is standing behind the lines, the race announcer yells, "One, two, three. Go." The first cowpuncher in each line puts on the boots and races across the room, takes off the boots, and gives them to the first cowpuncher waiting. Keep going until all the cowboys and cowgirls have shuffled in the boots. Yell "Yee Haw!" to the winning team.

Camp Cook Nicknames

Some cowboys, including camp cooks were secretive and never used their real names. Cooks were often given nicknames, such as "cookie" or "coosie." In the Southwest the Spanish name for a cook was *cocinero*. There were the not so nice nicknames too, such as "beanmaster," "belly-cheater," "grub-spoiler," "dough puncher," and "biscuit-shooter." Some nicknames came from events that happened. Others came from idiosyncracies or physical characteristics. Griping cooks, like many of them were, were given names like "Bellyache Bill" or "Sourdough Slim." Some of the "coosies" got back at the cowboys for name calling. One example was using dishwater to make the cowboys' beloved coffee. Drinking it, could bring on diarrhea. Most of the cooks were former cowboys. They probably had such poor humor because of their aches and pains. A smart cowboy treated the cook with respect and didn't enter the cook's territory between the chuck wagon and the fire without permission.

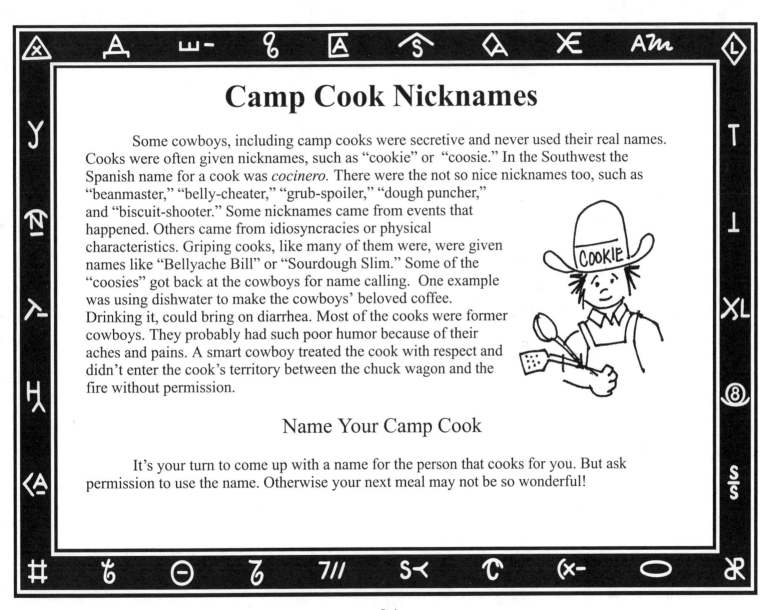

Name Your Camp Cook

It's your turn to come up with a name for the person that cooks for you. But ask permission to use the name. Otherwise your next meal may not be so wonderful!

Outlaw Hangouts

Search for your own "hangout." A "hangout" or "hide-out" as it was sometimes called, was a meeting place for rustlers and outlaws. Some hangouts were widely known. There was the Robbers' Roost in Utah, Hole in the Wall in Wyoming, Castle Rock in the Henry Mountains, and No Man's Land in Oklahoma.

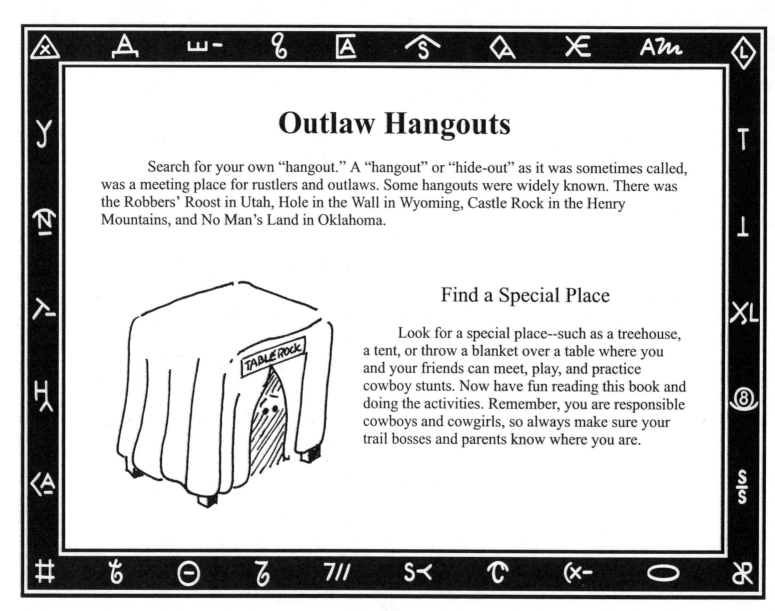

Find a Special Place

Look for a special place--such as a treehouse, a tent, or throw a blanket over a table where you and your friends can meet, play, and practice cowboy stunts. Now have fun reading this book and doing the activities. Remember, you are responsible cowboys and cowgirls, so always make sure your trail bosses and parents know where you are.

Horseback Riding

Few cowboys owned their own horses. The rancher owned them. But each cowboy had assigned a string of horses that were herded together with all the extra mounts in what was called the remuda. Cowboys loved riding horses. They spent more time in a saddle than on foot, usually about 10 to 14 hours a day. When riding, they felt as if they owned the world. Cowboys knew riding horseback could satisfy all their senses.

Ride 'em Cowboys

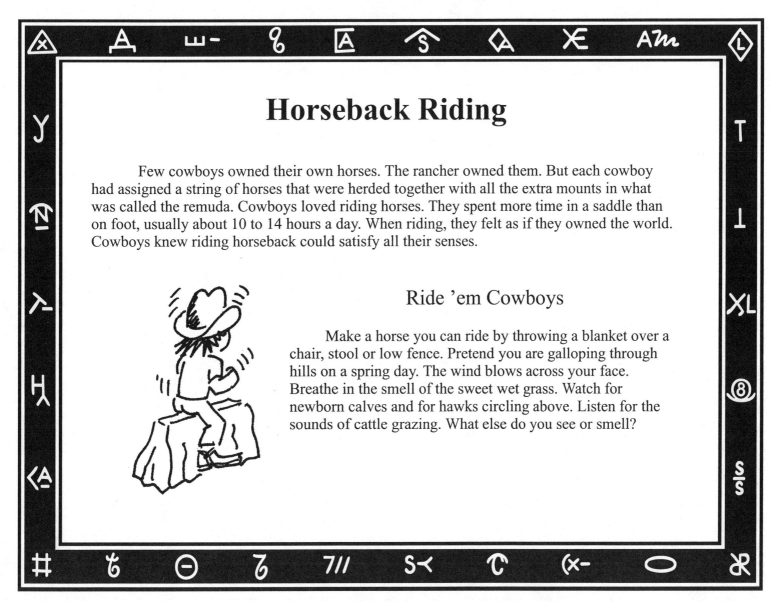

Make a horse you can ride by throwing a blanket over a chair, stool or low fence. Pretend you are galloping through hills on a spring day. The wind blows across your face. Breathe in the smell of the sweet wet grass. Watch for newborn calves and for hawks circling above. Listen for the sounds of cattle grazing. What else do you see or smell?

Cowboys Sing

Cowboys sang to quiet the cattle at night. They sang lullabies, hummed hymns, and sang of their troubles. Some songs were favorites and others were made up on the spot. The following song was made up.

Cowboy Slim.
Sprained his toe.
Following some buffalo.
Yippy-yi-yay!

Cowboy Slim.
Twisted his knee.
In a hole he didn't see.
Yippy-yi-yay!

Cowboy Slim.
Hurt his back.
Carrying a heavy pack.
Yippy-yi-yay!

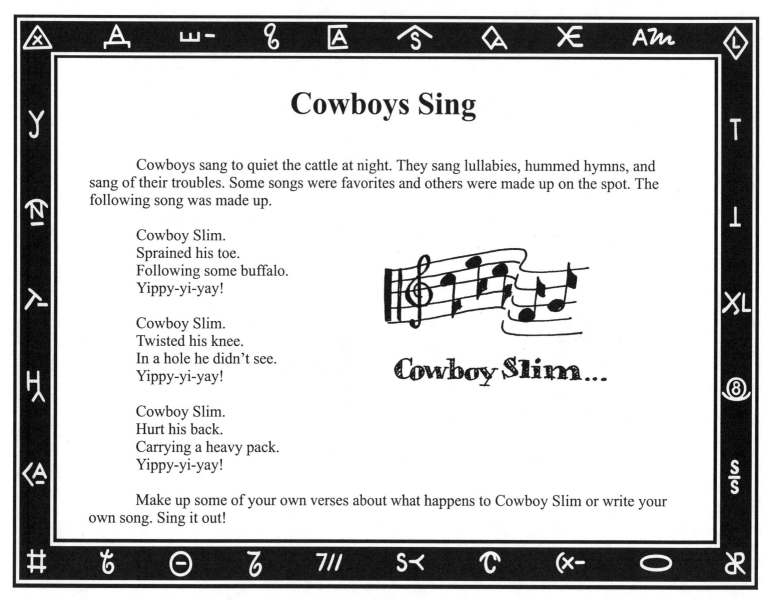

Make up some of your own verses about what happens to Cowboy Slim or write your own song. Sing it out!

Cowboys at Work

Cowboys work no matter what the weather or working conditions. They have to make sure the fences are mended, the calves are branded, sick cattle are doctored, and cattle are moved to and from the summer pasture. They work when it's hot and cold. They work in the pouring down rain and when the ground turns to mud.

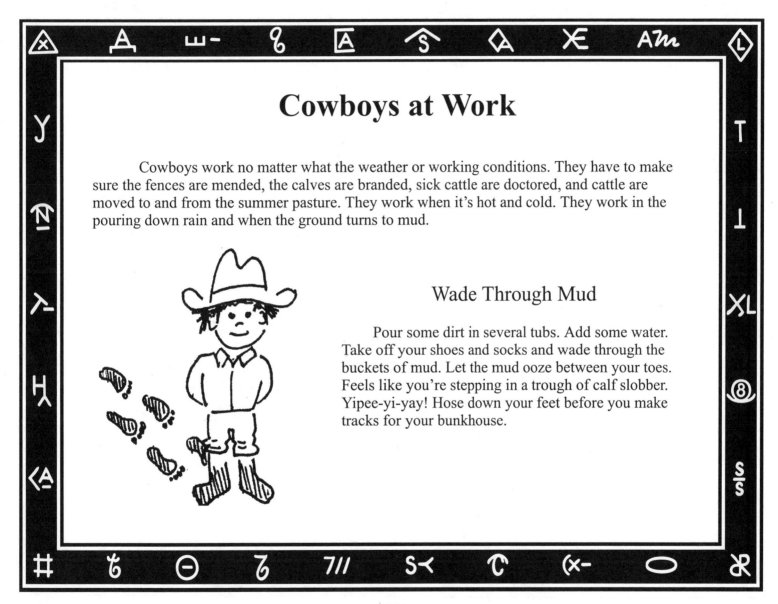

Wade Through Mud

Pour some dirt in several tubs. Add some water. Take off your shoes and socks and wade through the buckets of mud. Let the mud ooze between your toes. Feels like you're stepping in a trough of calf slobber. Yipee-yi-yay! Hose down your feet before you make tracks for your bunkhouse.

Cow Camp Etiquette

In a cow camp no one eats until "Cookie" calls. Cookie is a nickname given to cooks in the Old West. A good cook made good grub and was paid well. Cowboys had a lot of respect for the cook. No one talked back to the cook, or the chow might not be forthcoming. So, when Cookie called, the cowboys jumped up and grabbed their chow. They ate first and talked later. When they finished chowing down, they always put their dirty dishes in the wreck pan before they went back to work. Food left on a plate was an insult to Cookie.

Practice Cow Camp Etiquette

The above rules are good ones to follow on any range or in any kitchen. So, adjust these chuck wagon rules of etiquette to your situation, and follow them. For example, dirty dishes always go in the sink. Go to dinner when called, and remember, only a fool argues with the camp cook.

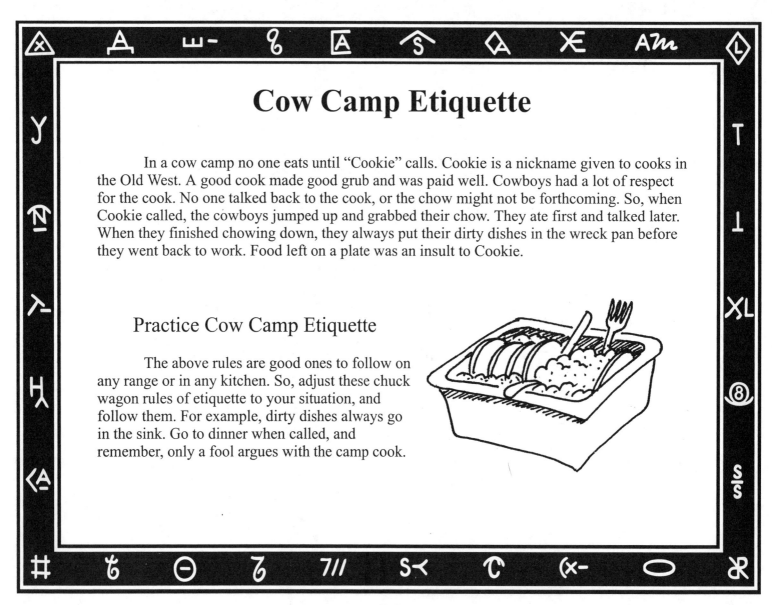

Cowboys Carry a Pannier

A pannier (pan´yer) is a container for carrying clothing and other supplies. Cowboys strapped them on packsaddles. One of these containers could be a bag or a box. The bag pannier was usually a flat sack made of canvas or leather. The box pannier was flat, narrow and covered with hide that still had the hair left on.

Make a Pannier

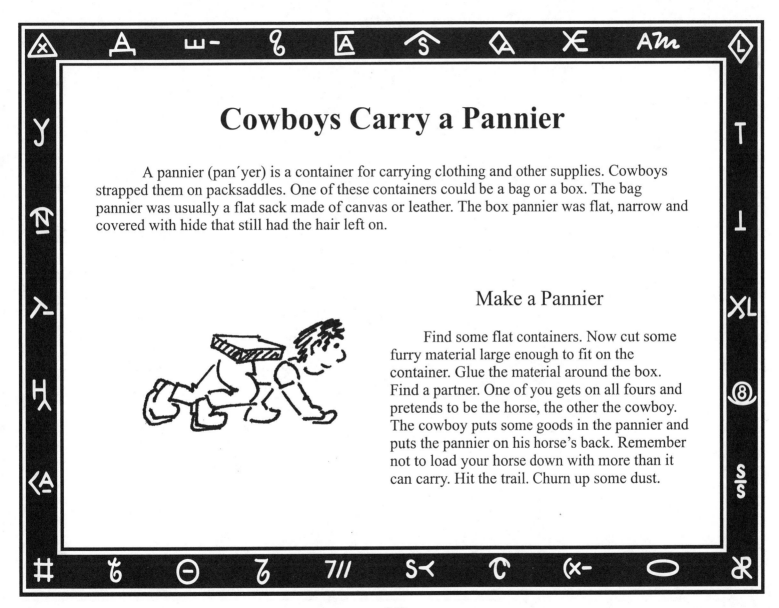

Find some flat containers. Now cut some furry material large enough to fit on the container. Glue the material around the box. Find a partner. One of you gets on all fours and pretends to be the horse, the other the cowboy. The cowboy puts some goods in the pannier and puts the pannier on his horse's back. Remember not to load your horse down with more than it can carry. Hit the trail. Churn up some dust.

A Cowboy's Horse

When buying a horse, a cowboy might first ask its name. Often times the horses were never named. A gray horse may have been called "the old gray mare." If horses were named, it was usually the bronc buster that named them while he broke them. Markings on the flesh or other characteristics were often used in the names, for example a horse with a star marking on it's forehead would be named Star. A horse with red hair would be named Red.

A Horse's Name

What would your horse look like or what characteristics would it have? Use these to name your horse. Do you know anyone with a horse? If so, find out how the horse came by his name.

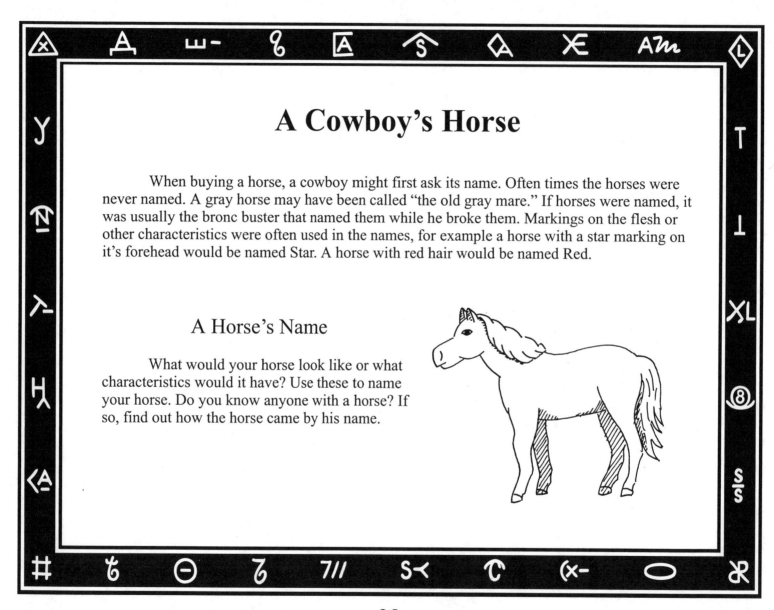

Barrel Racing

Barrel racing is much like cutting out cattle from a herd. A well-trained horse could turn sharply, stop quickly, frighten an animal from the herd, and keep it separated. In barrel racing, it takes lots of training for the horse and the rider to make the hairpin turns required in this race. The race is performed around three barrels set up in a triangular pattern. Two barrels are put at opposite sides in the center of a course. The third is placed across from the start. A judge drops a flag to signal the beginning of the race. The rider steers the horse around each barrel at least two turns in opposite directions, as horse and rider race against the clock. If the left barrel is taken first, that is a left turn, then horse and rider come across to the right barrel and make a right-handed turn, then proceed to the third barrel and make another right turn. If the right barrel is taken first, they have one right turn and two left turns. Much depends on whether the horse is left-footed or right-footed. A complete closed loop must be made around the barrel. If the horse goes on the wrong side, a complete loop is not created and the horse and rider are disqualified for "breaking the pattern." If a horse tips a barrel over, a five second penalty is assessed.

Have a Barrel Race

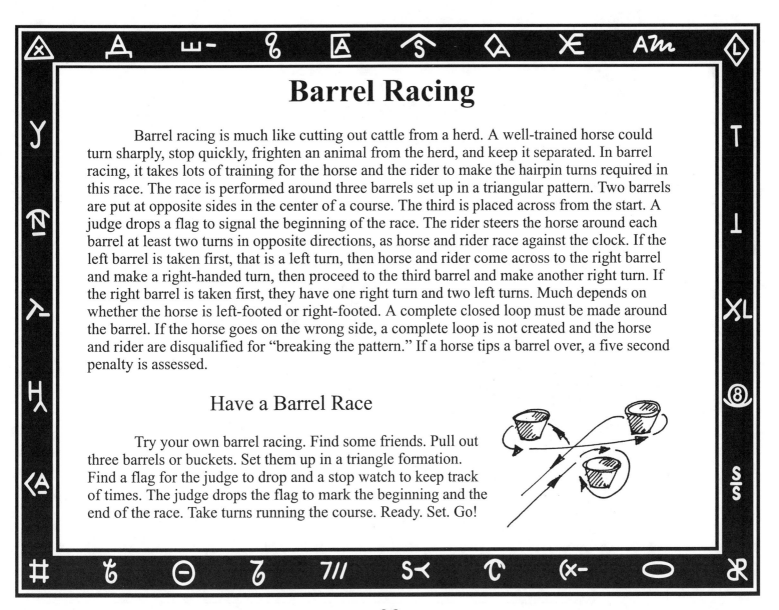

Try your own barrel racing. Find some friends. Pull out three barrels or buckets. Set them up in a triangle formation. Find a flag for the judge to drop and a stop watch to keep track of times. The judge drops the flag to mark the beginning and the end of the race. Take turns running the course. Ready. Set. Go!

Food for the Trail

Cowboys learned to make beef jerky from the Native Americans. The meat was cut into strips and placed on poles to dry. It took about three days in the sun to cure. Jerky meat doesn't spoil, so cowboys sometimes took it when they headed out on the trail or the range.

Make Beef Jerky

To make the jerky, start with a lean slab of beef. Partially freeze it to make it easier to cut. With adult help, cut the meat into long narrow strips about 1/4" thick. Sprinkle both sides of the meat with salt and pepper. Place the slices on a baking sheet in a single layer. Bake at 145° for about 6 hours. Check the meat now and then. Remove excess oil with a paper towel. If you're a true blue cowboy, use the old-time drying technique of hanging the meat from wires in the sun or some other warm dry place. The salt preserves it and the pepper keeps away any flying critters. Yeah, right! Now take that jerky on the trail. It should look and feel like leather, but tastes a might better.

The Rhythm of a Horse's Hooves

A horse walks in an even flat-footed four-beat gait. A trot is a two-beat gait. The horse's feet move in diagonal pairs. While two feet are in the air the other two are hitting the ground. It's also called a "jog." The canter is a three-beat gait. The horse leads out with one leg, then two legs move simultaneously, and finally the fourth leg strikes off last. This is a version of a gallop, a horse's natural running gait. It's a smooth succession of leaps. There's a brief moment when all four feet are off the ground at the same time.

Make the Rhythm of Your Horse's Hooves

Gather some friends. Find items that make a pounding noise, such as coconuts, rhythm sticks, or a couple of wood blocks. Hold one item in each hand. Use the items to sound like your horse's feet as they touch the ground. Now use the instruments to make the deafening roar of a herd of horses as they pass by.

Prairie Lawyers

A coyote is about the size of a medium-sized dog, weighing between 30 and 40 pounds. Coyotes are a gray-brown color with bushy tails. They are great runners, cruising at 25 to 30 miles per hour. For short distances they can go as fast as 40 miles per hour. The coyote can leap high fences. Cowboys consider them pests, because they occasionally attack livestock. Their distinctive barks, yelps, and howls can be heard from sundown to sunrise. Yip-yip-yahoo! Yip-yip-yahoo! Cowboys referred to them as prairie lawyers, because of this chatter. When celebrating, cowboys have been known to imitate the howl of the coyote.

Howl Like a Coyote

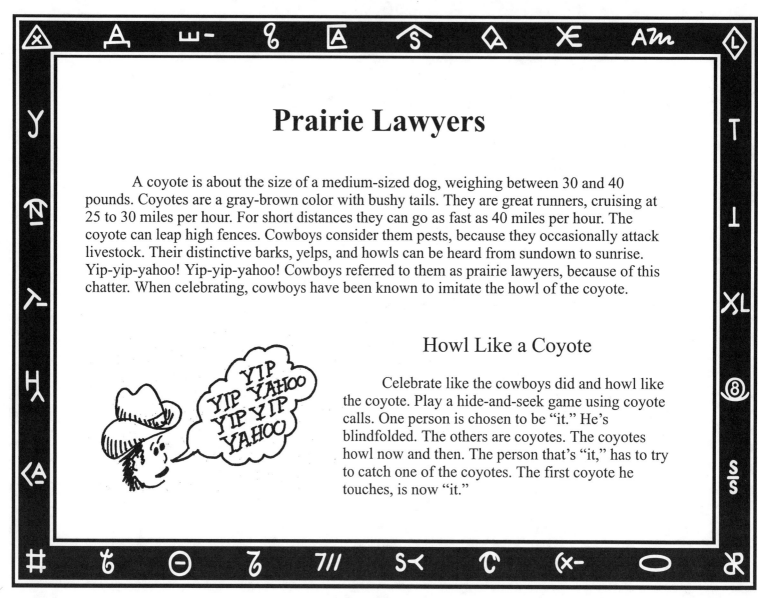

Celebrate like the cowboys did and howl like the coyote. Play a hide-and-seek game using coyote calls. One person is chosen to be "it." He's blindfolded. The others are coyotes. The coyotes howl now and then. The person that's "it," has to try to catch one of the coyotes. The first coyote he touches, is now "it."

The Cowboys' Storehouse

The chuck wagon was the cowboys' storehouse when they were rounding up cattle or driving them to markets. To make the chuck wagon into a kitchen, a hinged lid was let down to give the cook a work table, where he prepared the meals. But the chuck wagon served other functions as well, that of hospital, ranch office, and a hotel. The chuck wagon was designed to include cubbyholes and drawers for plenty of storage.

Packing the Chuck Wagon

What did cowboys need on the open range? Think of the supplies they needed for a month. Remember they needed to eat, drink, clean up, repair things, change clothing, bed down, be prepared for illnesses and injuries, and keep the cattle moving. Don't forget the weather conditions--rain, snow, and sun. Make a list and check it twice. Don't forget anything. Happy Trails!

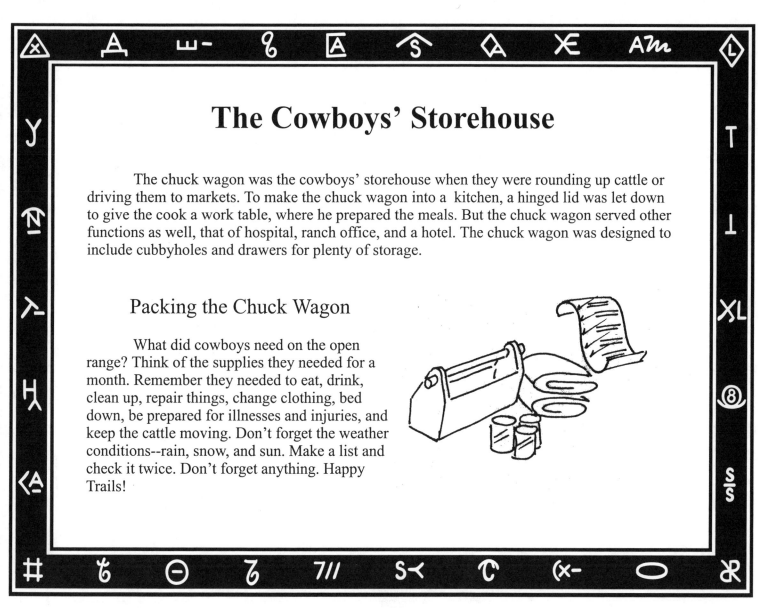

43

Cowboy Cuffs

Some cowboys wore cuffs to protect their wrists from injuries. Each cuff was a piece of stamped or carved leather decorated with conchas. A concha is a silver or metal disk that's been engraved or stamped. They are used to decorate cuffs, belts, bits, bridles and saddles. Cowboys laced or buckled the cuffs in place.

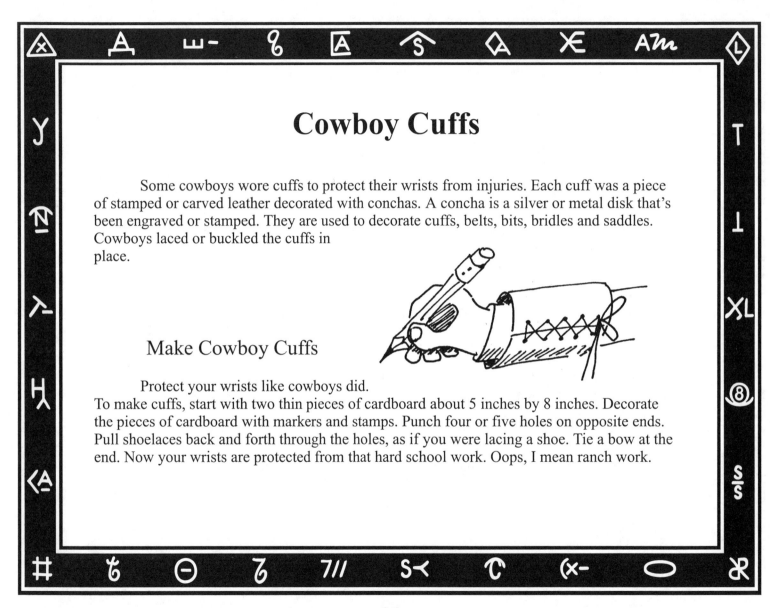

Make Cowboy Cuffs

Protect your wrists like cowboys did. To make cuffs, start with two thin pieces of cardboard about 5 inches by 8 inches. Decorate the pieces of cardboard with markers and stamps. Punch four or five holes on opposite ends. Pull shoelaces back and forth through the holes, as if you were lacing a shoe. Tie a bow at the end. Now your wrists are protected from that hard school work. Oops, I mean ranch work.

Sourdough Biscuits

Sourdough biscuits were a staple in most cow camps. The cook had to have sourdough starter to make the biscuits. He stored the starter inside the wagon box to keep it warm, so the yeast could work. On especially cold nights, he slept with it. To make sourdough starter you need:

2 medium potatoes
3 cups water
2 cups flour
1 tablespoon sugar

Peel the potatoes. With adult help, cut the potatoes into small cubes. Boil them in the water. When the potatoes are tender, remove the pot from the stove. You don't need the potatoes. Pour the potato water in a bowl. After the water has cooled, add the flour and the sugar. Mix well. Cover the mixture and put it in a warm place for several days, so the dough can rise. Recipe for the biscuits:

3-4 cups flour
1 cup sourdough starter
1 teaspoon salt
1 teaspoon sugar
1 teaspoon baking soda
1 tablespoon shortening

Sift the flour in a bowl. Make a well in the center. Add the sourdough starter. Stir in the salt, sugar and baking soda. Add the shortening. Mix enough flour with the ingredients to make a stiff dough. Roll the dough into balls, and dip them in melted shortening. Place the balls on an 8-inch cake pan and let them sit in a warm place for 20-30 minutes. Bake at 425° for approximately 12 minutes or until light brown.

Hope you're hungrier than a wolf after guts so you eat them right away. The day after they were baked, one cowboy said the biscuits were so hard, they made his teeth hurt.

A Cowboy Knows His Horse

A cowboy watches his horse carefully and knows what's on his horse's mind. In particular, he observes her eyes and ears. When the ears are forward, the horse is paying attention. Drooping ears mean the horse is not paying attention. Be sure to get her attention, before touching her. Relaxed ears mean the horse is relaxed, so the cowboy can relax too, because she is less likely to spook. When the ears are pointing back, the horse may be listening to the rider or to something coming up from behind, but ears pinned back against the neck means the cowboy should back off. An angry horse might bite or kick.

How's Your Partner Feeling?

Think of ways people show emotions. Grab a partner. One of you will use facial expressions and gestures to show the following emotions: anger, happiness, sadness, and fear. The partner guesses what emotion is being shown. Trade roles and do this activity again.

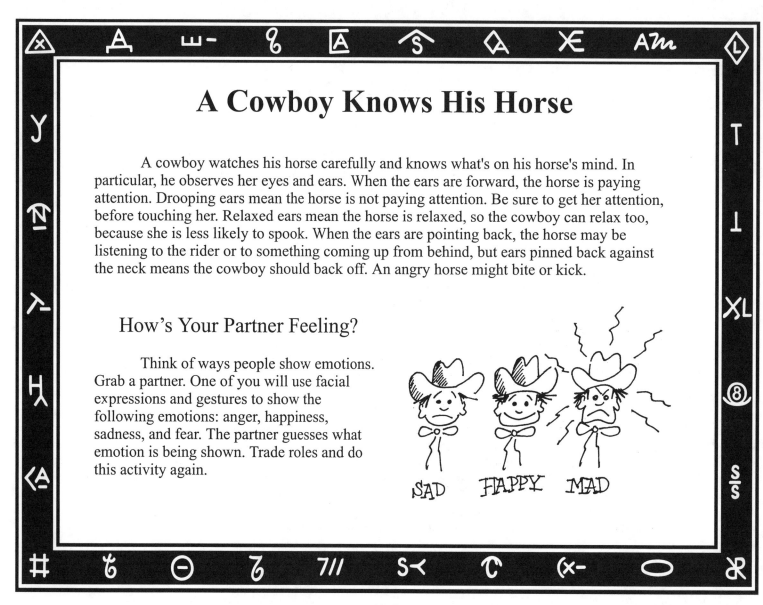

SAD HAPPY MAD

Branding Irons

A brand showed ownership of an animal. Each rancher had his own symbol. In the old days there were fewer fences, and the cattle roamed, so a couple of times a year, each rancher rounded up his cattle and branded the new calves. This mark was made by heating a branding iron and using it to burn a pattern of hair on the animal's flank. The rancher's design was fashioned by a blacksmith and soldered onto the end of the iron. This was called a fixed branding iron. A running iron was more like a fire poker. Rustlers used this iron to change brands, so it became illegal to carry one.

Make a Fixed Branding Iron

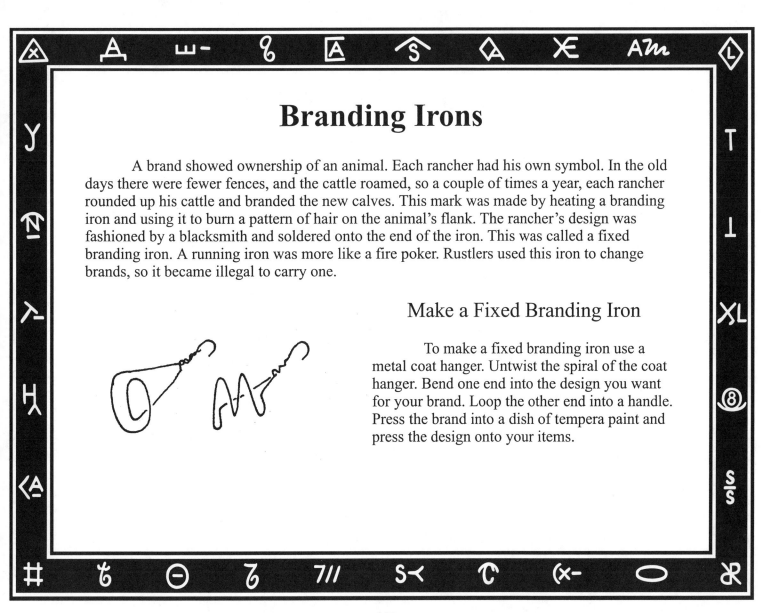

To make a fixed branding iron use a metal coat hanger. Untwist the spiral of the coat hanger. Bend one end into the design you want for your brand. Loop the other end into a handle. Press the brand into a dish of tempera paint and press the design onto your items.

Cowboy Road Rules

Most cowboys were law-abiding young men who followed unwritten road rules. If an honest cowboy spotted stray livestock, he'd chase them back into the field they came from. If he was too far from home, he would get ahold of the owner to let him know his cattle had strayed. A cowboy always waved at others, whether he knew them or not. A cowboy took the time to chew the fat with friends and neighbors he met on the road. In other words, most cowboys were friendly and all around decent dudes.

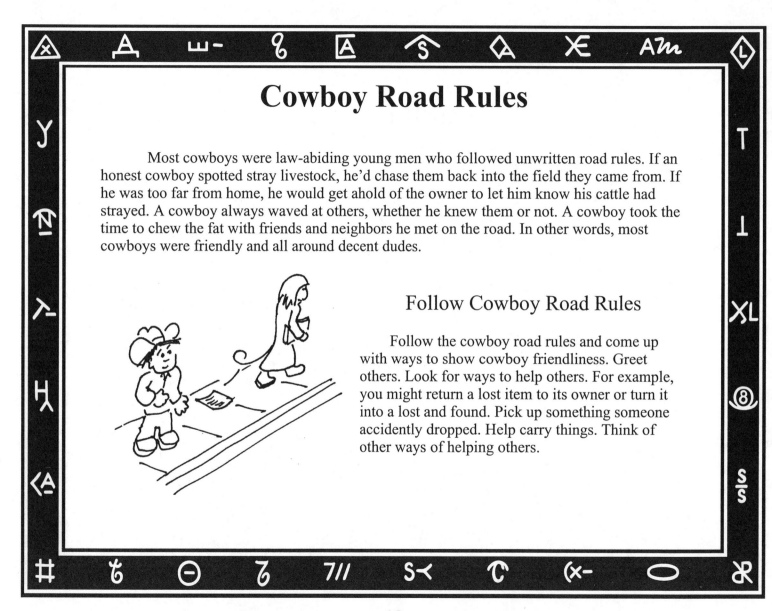

Follow Cowboy Road Rules

Follow the cowboy road rules and come up with ways to show cowboy friendliness. Greet others. Look for ways to help others. For example, you might return a lost item to its owner or turn it into a lost and found. Pick up something someone accidently dropped. Help carry things. Think of other ways of helping others.

A Bull and His Rider

   During a rodeo, the bull rider gets a lot of attention, and if he wins, plenty of yahoos. A bull rider could write pages on the thrill of riding in the rodeo circuit. A hotshot bull rider could write a résumé, a list of his accomplishments, to land a job. The bulls earn a reputation and are rated too. Mean bulls are in demand, because a cowboy can earn more points by staying on a mean bull.

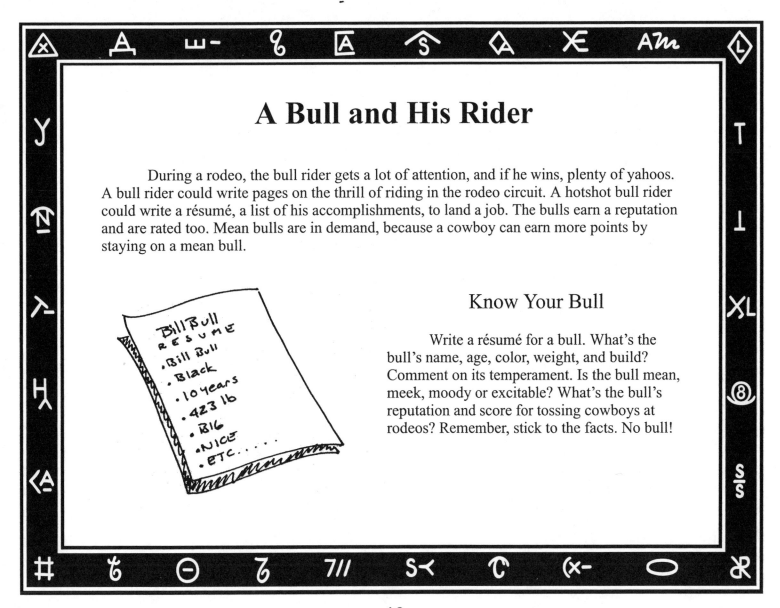

Know Your Bull

   Write a résumé for a bull. What's the bull's name, age, color, weight, and build? Comment on its temperament. Is the bull mean, meek, moody or excitable? What's the bull's reputation and score for tossing cowboys at rodeos? Remember, stick to the facts. No bull!

Pioneer Weights and Measures

Cow camp cooks didn't necessarily do much measuring or use recipes, but the pioneer women did. They were experts in their kitchens and cranked out some tasty foods. Here are some examples of pioneer weights and measures:

► Twenty-five drops of liquid will fill one common teaspoon.
► Three teaspoonfuls equals one tablespoon.
► Sixteen tablespoons equals one coffee cupful or eight ounces.
► Two coffee cupfuls equals one pint and weighs one pound.
► Two tablespoons liquid equals one liquid ounce.
► One-eighth teaspoon is a pinch.
► Four coffee cupfuls of liquid equals one quart.
► An ordinary tumblerful (8 ounces) equals one coffee cupful or half a pint.

Do Some Measurin'

Find a dropper, teaspoons, tablespoons, cups, and a scale. Experiment with these weights and measures to see if they really work. Put on your cow camp apron and use the weights and measures in some recipes.

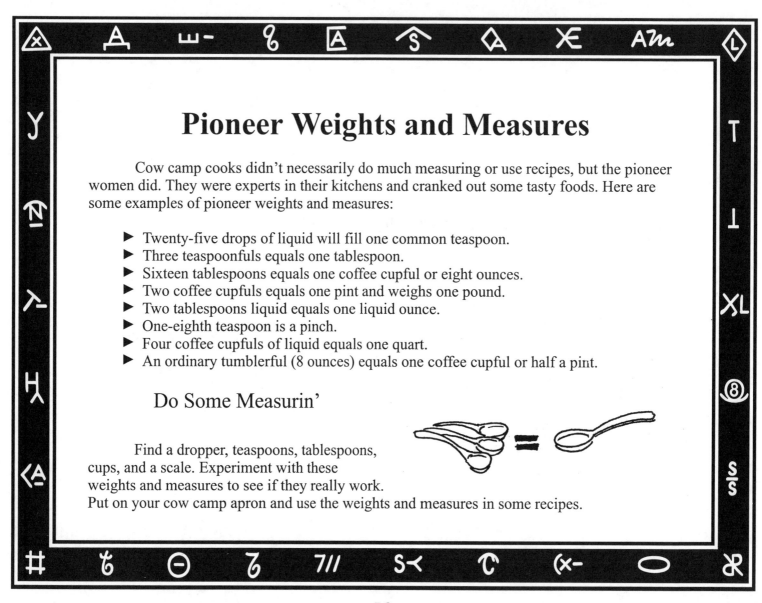

Old-Time Characters

The West was full of good cowboys and outlaws. Here are a couple of examples.

Lucyle Garner Richards was abandoned by her parents at age twelve. That's when she rode to an Indian boarding school that she attended and where she worked as a dishwasher. A year later she was riding in a rodeo. She went on to work in a wild west show and even had a stage name. She strived for excellence in areas that interested her. Her goal was to become a world-renowned cowgirl.

Sam Bass started as a handy man for a sheriff. He went on to race his horse "Denton Mare." His mare was faster than other horses. After some fishy races in Mexico, he sold his horse and drove cattle to Kansas for a rancher. Sam and his partner sold the cattle and spent the money. Then he began robbing stage coaches. Sam had become an outlaw. They say he could carve his initials on a tree trunk while riding past on his horse.

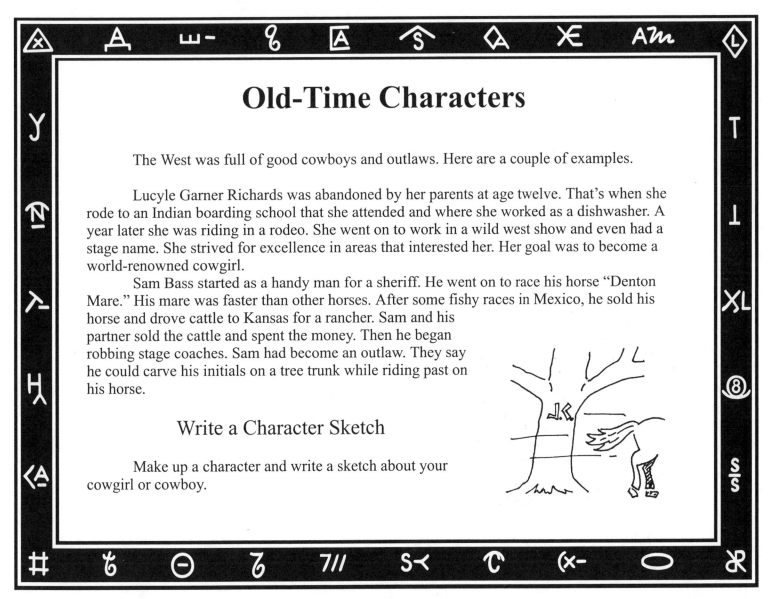

Write a Character Sketch

Make up a character and write a sketch about your cowgirl or cowboy.

Buffalo and Cow Chips

Beneath the chuck wagon hung a "cooney" or dried cowhide. Cowboys used it to carry firewood and chips. These chips were sun-dried manure left by the buffalo or cattle. While riding on treeless plains, no wood could be found. Buffalo chips became prized possessions. Cowboys burned the chips for fuel. The chips made a hot, blue flame. Follow the recipe below to make some buffalo chips you can eat.

Ingredients:
- ► 2 cups dirt chunks (chocolate chips)
- ► 1 tablespoon buffalo fat (shortening)
- ► ½ cup shriveled beans (raisins)
- ► ½ cup rocks (pistachios)
- ► Sprinkling of trail dust (powdered sugar)

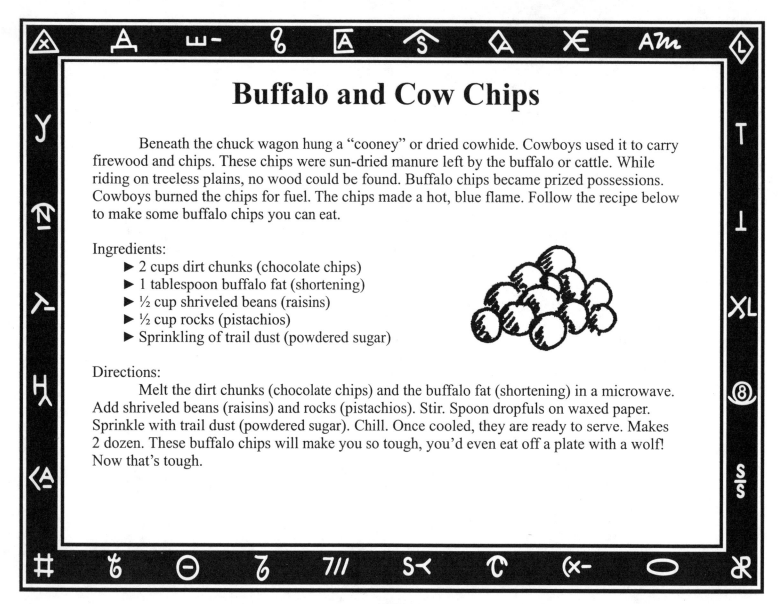

Directions:
Melt the dirt chunks (chocolate chips) and the buffalo fat (shortening) in a microwave. Add shriveled beans (raisins) and rocks (pistachios). Stir. Spoon dropfuls on waxed paper. Sprinkle with trail dust (powdered sugar). Chill. Once cooled, they are ready to serve. Makes 2 dozen. These buffalo chips will make you so tough, you'd even eat off a plate with a wolf! Now that's tough.

Roping

Every cowboy had to learn to throw a rope to catch an animal. It was a skill needed during roundups and for most cattle work. Until a young cowboy mastered roping, his job on the roundups was to keep the herds close by or the cattle cut, separated. A cowboy had to be able to throw a rope while on foot and when mounted on a horse. The rope was an extension of the cowboy.

So You Want to be a Roper

Here's a checklist of what it takes to be a top notch roper. See how you do. A roper:

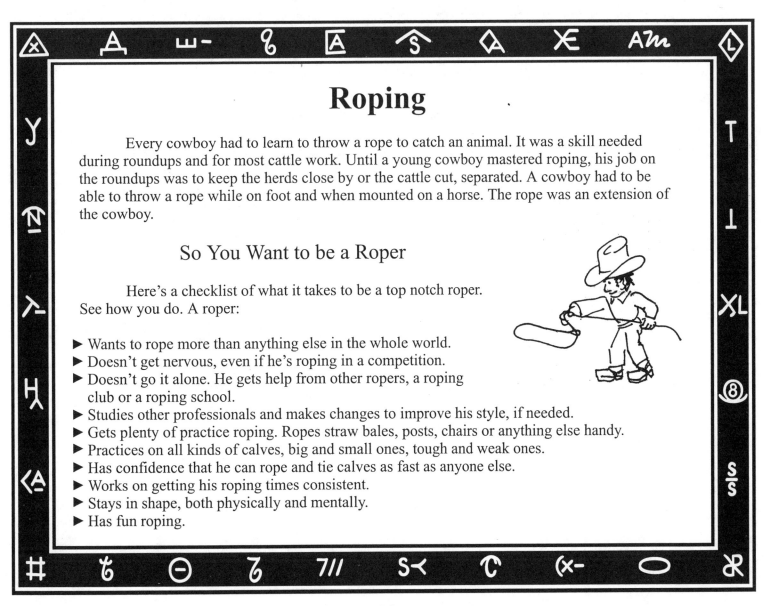

- ▶ Wants to rope more than anything else in the whole world.
- ▶ Doesn't get nervous, even if he's roping in a competition.
- ▶ Doesn't go it alone. He gets help from other ropers, a roping club or a roping school.
- ▶ Studies other professionals and makes changes to improve his style, if needed.
- ▶ Gets plenty of practice roping. Ropes straw bales, posts, chairs or anything else handy.
- ▶ Practices on all kinds of calves, big and small ones, tough and weak ones.
- ▶ Has confidence that he can rope and tie calves as fast as anyone else.
- ▶ Works on getting his roping times consistent.
- ▶ Stays in shape, both physically and mentally.
- ▶ Has fun roping.

Cowboys are Weather-Wise

Cattle must be tended regardless of the weather. Cowboys work when it's pouring down rain, in scorching heat, during a gale wind, and in near-blizzard conditions. This explains why they talk about the weather. A cowboy might look at the sky and say, "This could really turn into something." They watch for signs that give them clues about the weather, such as restless animals and wildlife heading downhill. Distant sounds that are loud and sharp could mean rain, as does a change in wind direction, and leaves that turn over and show their bottom sides. Clouds with hard edges could mean strong winds. On the prairies, clouds with a greenish cast might bring hail.

Cowboy Weatherman

Go outside and check out the land and the skies. Do you see any telltale signs that mean the weather might change? Make a weather forecast. Keep checking the weather. Was your prediction right?

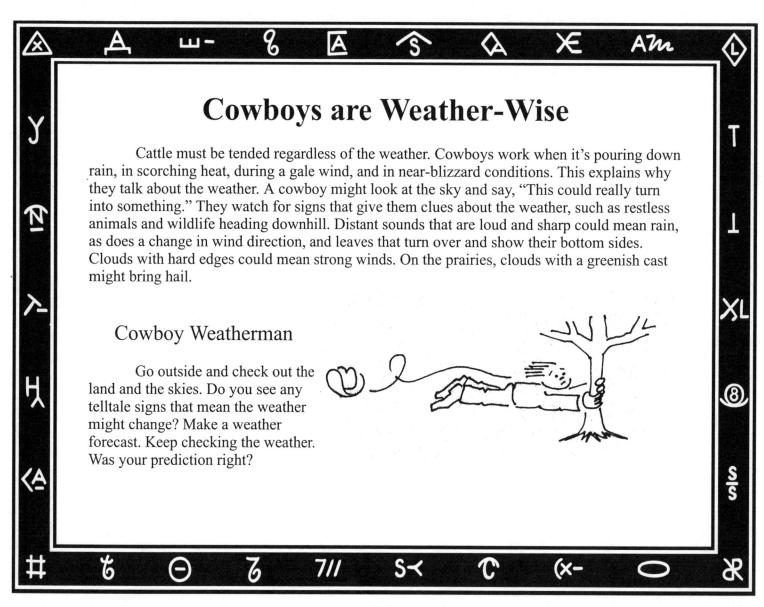

Read Brands

Many brands were made from single capital letters, but there were several ways to make the letters. Some of the letters cowboys used in their brands had wings, made with squiggles one on each side of a letter at the top. Other letters looked like they were being dragged along on the ground. They added lines angled down toward the left from letters to look like they were leaving a trail behind them. Some brands contained letters that looked like they were walking. This was done by adding feet to the letters. Running letters looked similar to cursive letters, because they looked like you didn't pick up the pencil while writing them. Letters would tumble, which meant they were tipped over. They could be reversed too.

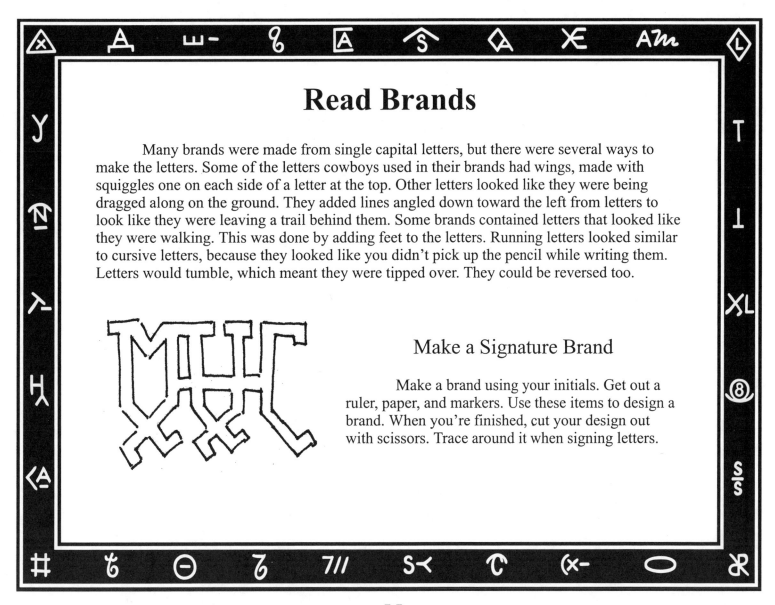

Make a Signature Brand

Make a brand using your initials. Get out a ruler, paper, and markers. Use these items to design a brand. When you're finished, cut your design out with scissors. Trace around it when signing letters.

Cowboy Range Prayers

There were some religious practices on the range. Songs sung by cowboys included hymns. A cowboy who could read might carry a Bible. And sometimes cowboys prayed before they ate. Here are a couple of their prayers.

Eat your meat and save the skin;
Turn up your plates and let's begin.

Thar's the bread, thar's the meat;
Now, by Joe, let's eat.

Say a Cowboy Prayer

Make up a prayer that a cowboy might say. Be sure to say it before eating. Then chow down.

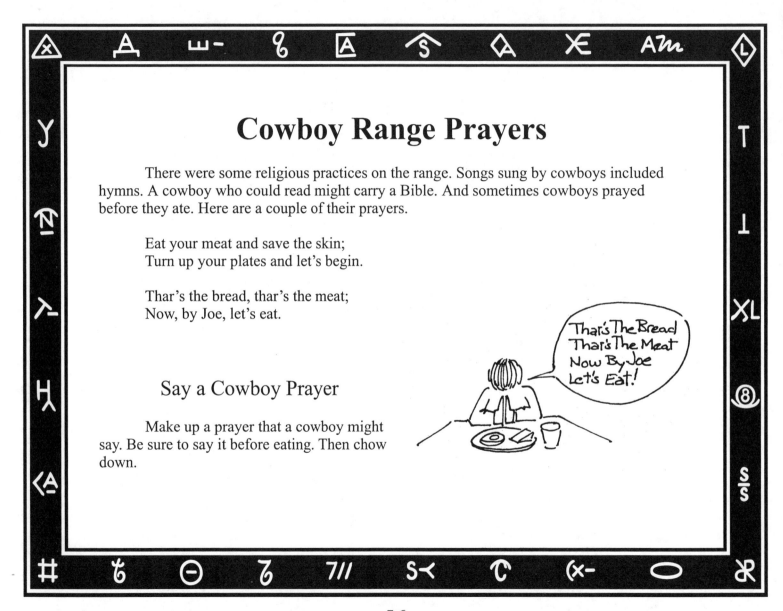

The Old Chisholm Trail

Many cowboys sang and rode the Old Chisholm Trail. By the way, it's pronounced Chizzum. This was a widely sung song by the cowboys. It gives all the possible scenarios for a group of cowboys driving a herd of cattle from Texas to Dodge City. I hear tell there are a thousand verses and various versions. It starts like this:

> Come along, boys, and listen to my tale. I'll
> tell you all my troubles on the old Chisholm trail.

The refrain goes like this.

> Com-a ti yi you-py you-py yea, you-py yea,
> Com-a ti yi you-py you-py yea.

Write Verses to the Old Chisholm Trail

Write your own verses to the Old Chisholm Trail. Think about all the woes the cowboys faced on a long trail ride. They might lose their hats in strong winds, become weary of eating beans, a hoss might go lame, cattle might stray and have to be rounded up, or a stampede could occur. The cowboys might freeze or not find water. Sometimes cowboys threatened to quit and go into farming. Get busy and write. Then sing them out! Com-a ti yi you-py you-py yea.

A Cowboy Needs Shelter

     While out on a trail, a cowboy sometimes needed a temporary shelter for the night, called a wickiup or lean-to. He could make a wickiup by placing poles against a cross-bar and covering them with a blanket or tarpaulin. A hill helped make a handy shelter too, because he could lean the poles against the side of the hill.

Make a Wickiup

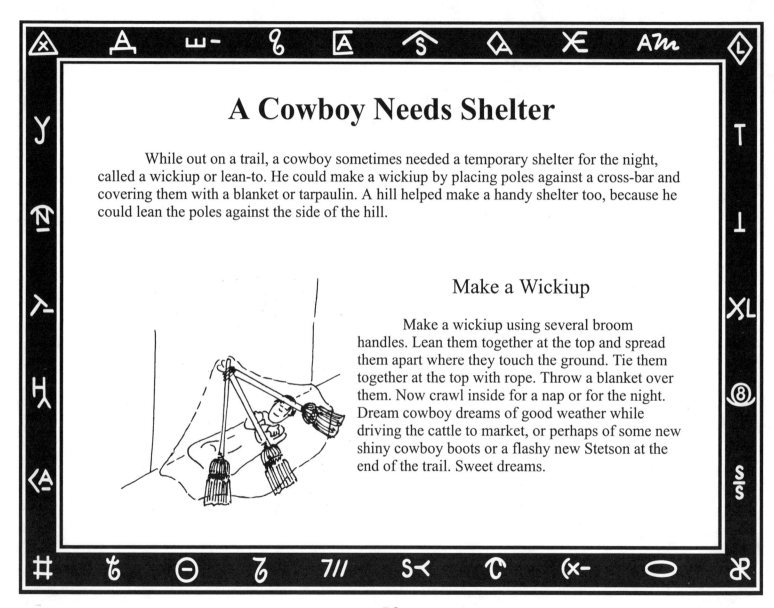

     Make a wickiup using several broom handles. Lean them together at the top and spread them apart where they touch the ground. Tie them together at the top with rope. Throw a blanket over them. Now crawl inside for a nap or for the night. Dream cowboy dreams of good weather while driving the cattle to market, or perhaps of some new shiny cowboy boots or a flashy new Stetson at the end of the trail. Sweet dreams.

Frying-Pan Bread

Old-time cowboys made frying-pan bread with flour, water, and baking powder. After a frying pan warmed over hot coals, the cookie poured a thin layer of batter into it. When a crust formed on the bottom, he tipped the pan on its side, so the rising heat could reach the dough and raise the loaf. To make some frying-pan bread you need:

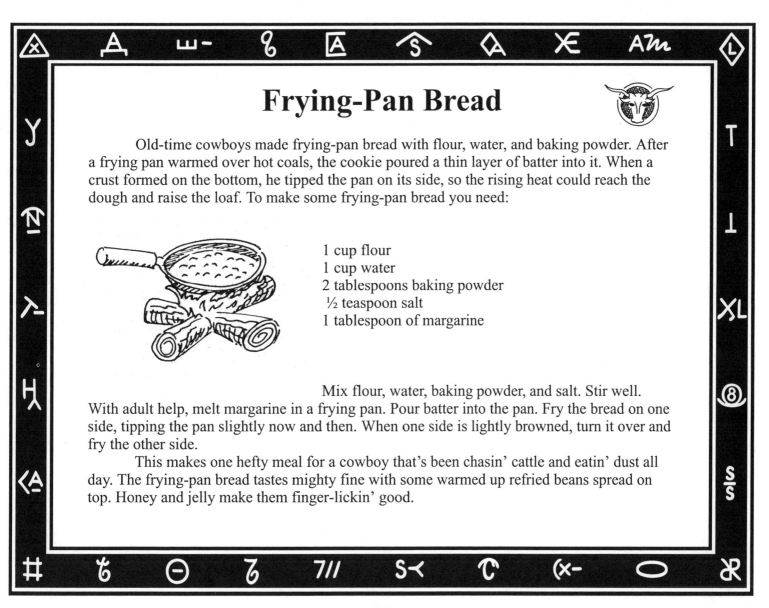

1 cup flour
1 cup water
2 tablespoons baking powder
½ teaspoon salt
1 tablespoon of margarine

Mix flour, water, baking powder, and salt. Stir well. With adult help, melt margarine in a frying pan. Pour batter into the pan. Fry the bread on one side, tipping the pan slightly now and then. When one side is lightly browned, turn it over and fry the other side.

This makes one hefty meal for a cowboy that's been chasin' cattle and eatin' dust all day. The frying-pan bread tastes mighty fine with some warmed up refried beans spread on top. Honey and jelly make them finger-lickin' good.

Cowboys Talk to Their Horses

How do you command a horse? Cowboys use physical signals to communicate with their horses. Cowboys say, "Even an unschooled horse can learn to follow commands." A touch to the side of the horse with the cowboy's legs or his spurs, gets the horse moving. Knees and reins, as well as spurs, cue the horse to turn. Tugging on reins pulls at the bit in the horse's mouth, which tells him to stop. Conditioning a horse takes repetition of commands followed by rewards.

Talk to Your Horse

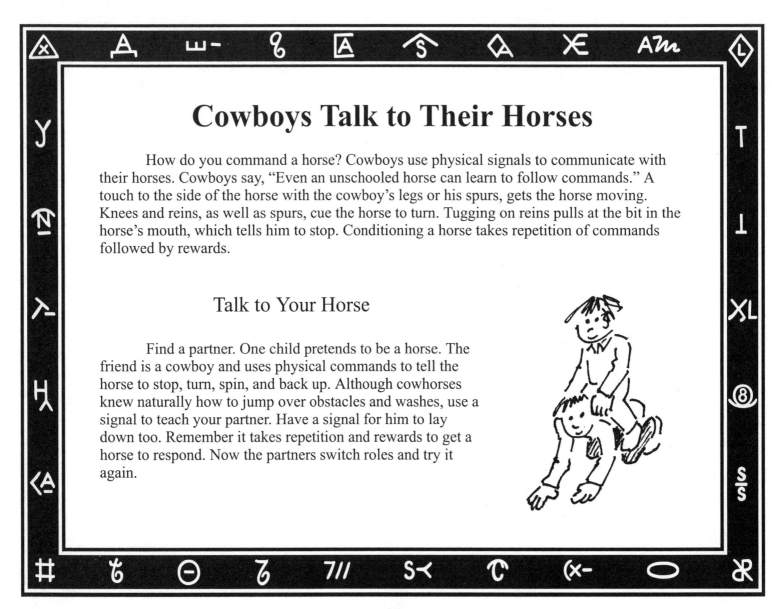

Find a partner. One child pretends to be a horse. The friend is a cowboy and uses physical commands to tell the horse to stop, turn, spin, and back up. Although cowhorses knew naturally how to jump over obstacles and washes, use a signal to teach your partner. Have a signal for him to lay down too. Remember it takes repetition and rewards to get a horse to respond. Now the partners switch roles and try it again.

Goin' to Town

Getting into the nearest town took time, because the nearest town could be a long ways away. The roads were rough too. When cowboys and cowgirls ventured to town, they usually bought a month's supply or more of provisions. In addition to food, they purchased items they needed to run the ranch and some personal items too.

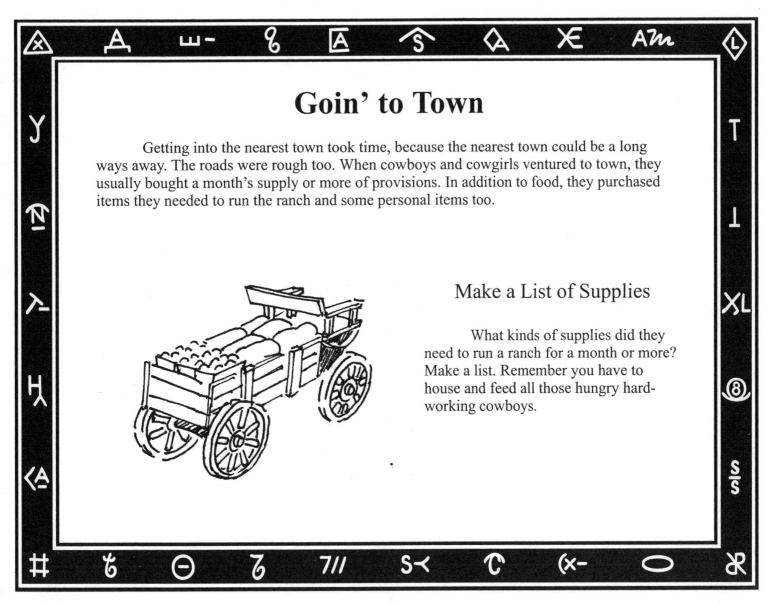

Make a List of Supplies

What kinds of supplies did they need to run a ranch for a month or more? Make a list. Remember you have to house and feed all those hungry hard-working cowboys.

Cowboys Take Care of Their Ropes

Ropes were expensive, so a cowboy always took good care of his rope. He kept it clean and free of mud and grease. If his rope got damp, he would let it dry before putting it away. A cowboy knew it was a good idea to wash his rope once a year. He never threw his rope into a corner, but instead, stored it where it would be immediately available for his use.

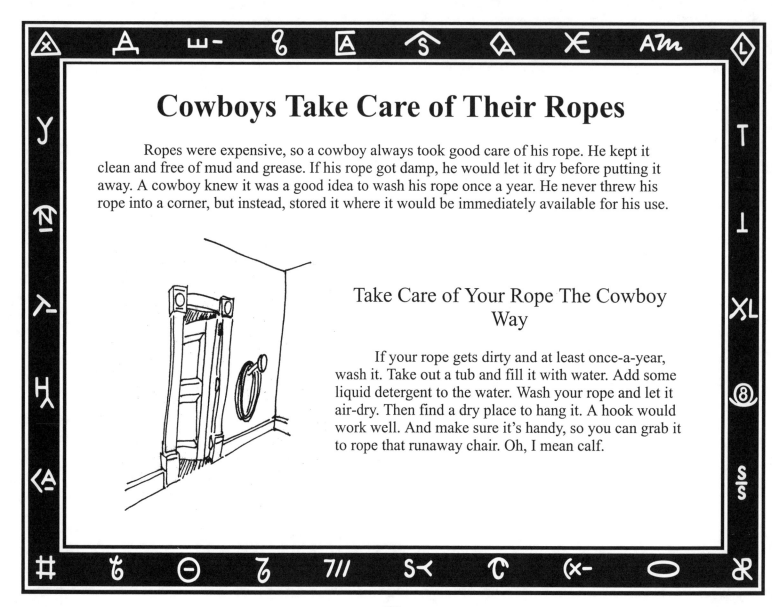

Take Care of Your Rope The Cowboy Way

If your rope gets dirty and at least once-a-year, wash it. Take out a tub and fill it with water. Add some liquid detergent to the water. Wash your rope and let it air-dry. Then find a dry place to hang it. A hook would work well. And make sure it's handy, so you can grab it to rope that runaway chair. Oh, I mean calf.

Gittin' Some Water

Sometimes a cowboy had to rig up a "go-devil" to get a drink of water. A go-devil helped scoop water out of a stream with high banks. A wire was stretched from the top of a bank and anchored into the stream. Then a rope was attached to a bucket that traveled back and forth along the wire. It was lowered into the stream empty and pulled up full.

Make a Go-Devil

Take a metal coat hanger apart and bend each end around to form two hooks. Knot a piece of rope onto one end. Hook the other end of the coat hanger wire onto the handle of a small bucket. With the rope, lower the bucket into some water. Now pull it up full.

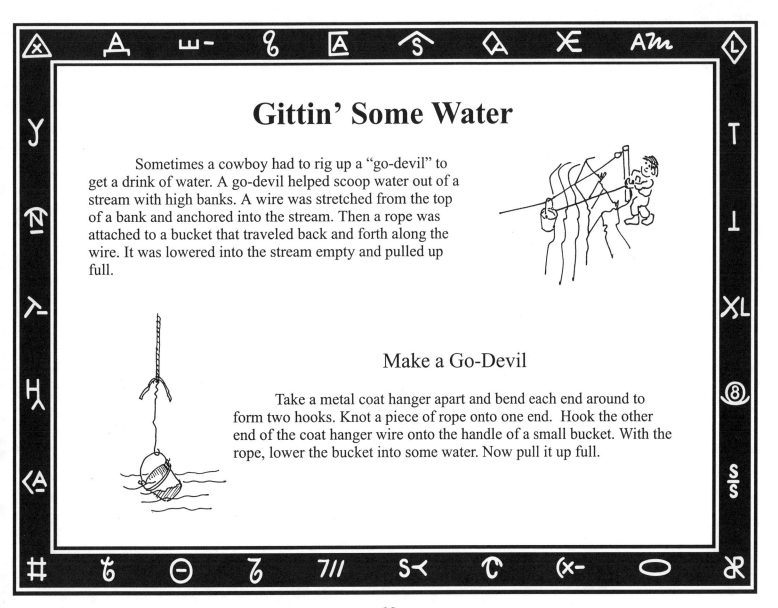

Cowboys Sing Out

Cowboys often sang while they worked. On the trail, they rode around their herds singing, because they believed it soothed the nervous cattle. They sang to the stars and the girls they left behind. Some of the songs were popular at the time. Others they "made up." Sometimes ranches had neighboring singing marathons when work was slack. These marathons lasted several nights. Each ranch sent their best singing cowboy. Cowboys took turns singing. The last man singing knew the most songs "by heart."

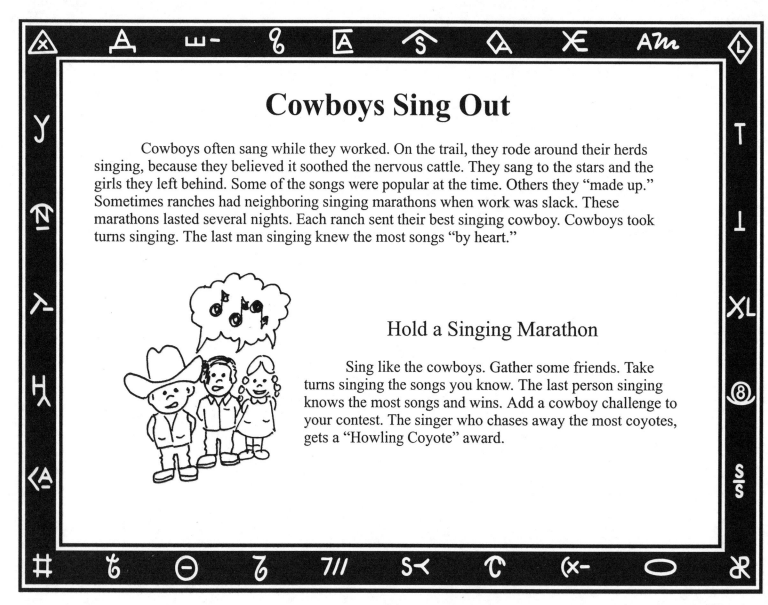

Hold a Singing Marathon

Sing like the cowboys. Gather some friends. Take turns singing the songs you know. The last person singing knows the most songs and wins. Add a cowboy challenge to your contest. The singer who chases away the most coyotes, gets a "Howling Coyote" award.

Cowboy Gloves

Some cowboys didn't wear gloves, so their hands were weathered, scarred, and tanned from ranch work. But other cowboys wore gloves, so their hands were soft and white. In cold weather, gloves kept their hands warm, and in warm weather, cowboys wore gloves while roping or riding bucking broncos. Gloves were usually made from horsehide or buckskin and most often were brown, but could be yellow, gray, creamy white or a greenish color. Some old-time cowboys wore fringed gloves decorated with the Lone Star, the symbol for Texas.

Lone Star Gloves

To make the gloves, start with a plain pair of gloves. Cut two stars from fabric and glue them onto the top side of each glove. For the fringe, cut two rectangular pieces of material. To get the right size, measure from the open end of the glove to where the small finger starts. Now make straight parallel cuts, fringing the material. With needle and thread, sew each piece of material along the underside of the glove or ask you trail boss to hot glue it. Wear your gloves to do your chores.

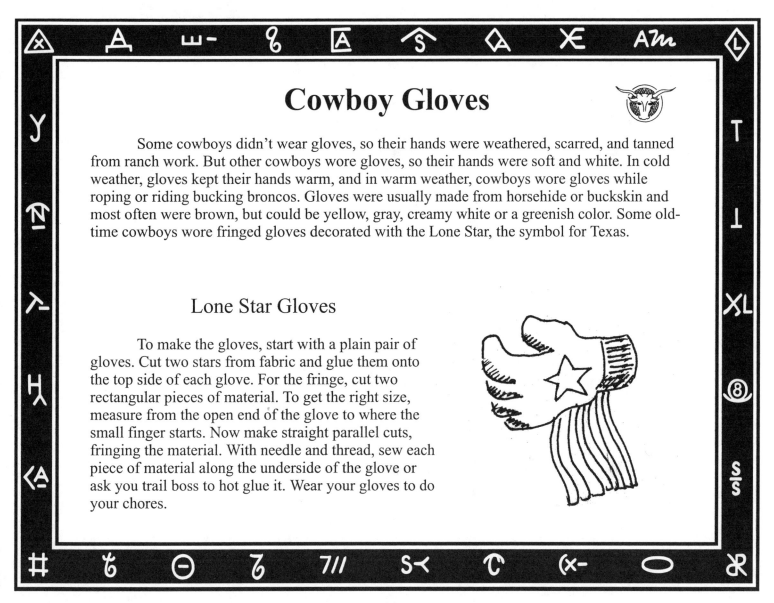

The Cowboy's Bed

The cowboys had to endure periods of cold weather. When they bedded down for the night, they made a bedroll from a pair of blankets or quilts. They wrapped them in a canvas groundsheet for protection from rain and snow. North of the Platte River, they were called "suggan" or "hot roll." During the day, the cowboys threw them into the chuck wagon or a lone cowboy strapped it onto his saddle.

Make a Cowboy Bedroll

To make a bedroll, use two blankets. Lay one blanket flat on the ground and lay the second one on top. Place it a little higher than the first one, until about three inches of the first blanket shows at the bottom. Fold the top blanket in thirds. Pin down the free edge with several large safety pins. Fold the bottom blanket around the top one and secure with several safety pins. Beginning on the top end, roll the blankets. Secure them with belts. Throw your bedroll over your shoulder. Take it outside. Lay it on the ground and climb inside. Now snooze. Zzz . . .

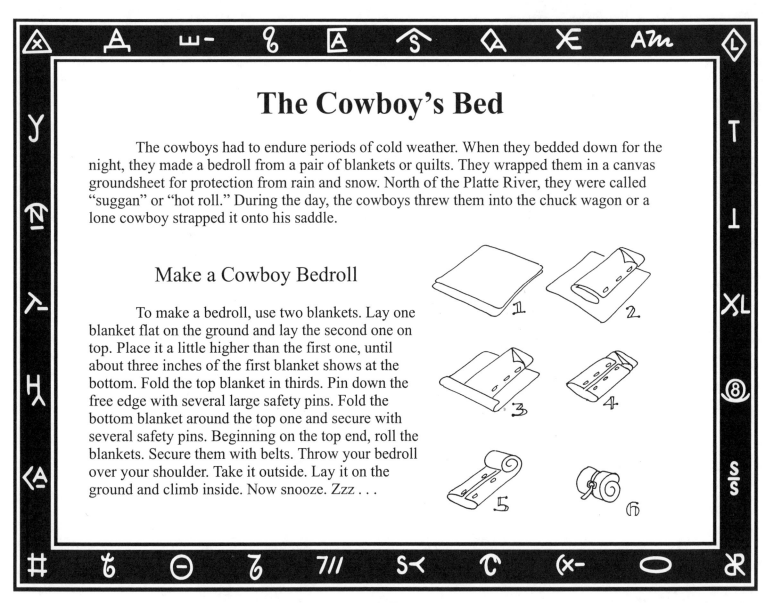

An Unruly Horse

Often cowboys didn't need to tie up their horses, because they had them so well trained. When they dropped the reins, the horse stayed put. But this wasn't always the case. Some horses seemed to have a competitive streak, an "I don't want to lose" attitude. These horses might test their riders and try to get away with things. A cowboy with an unruly horse would tie his horse to a hitching post.

Tie Up Your Horse

To tie up your horse, you need to know how to make a hitching post knot. Begin by looping your rope around a fence post. Pull on the loose end of the rope, threading it over itself, and tucking the end up through the loop you've just made. Pull the end of the rope through the second loop. Pull to tighten the knot.

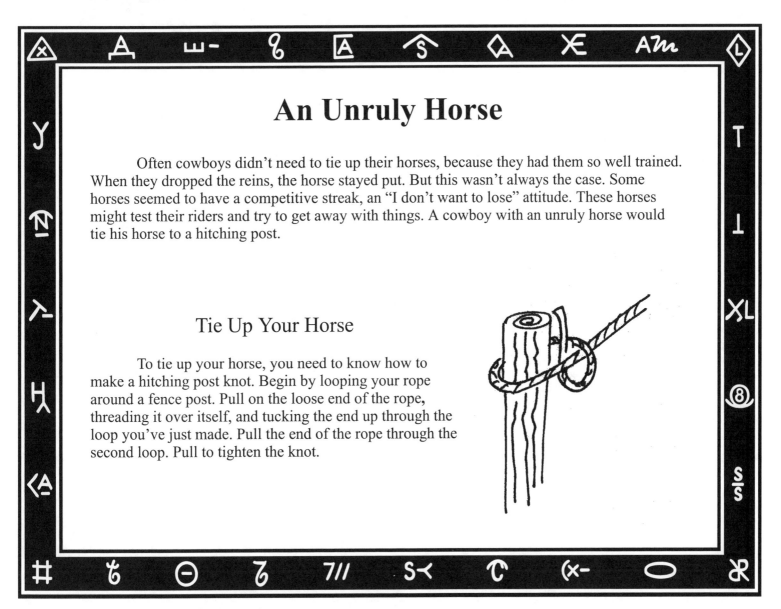

Talented Cooks

Cooks ran the gamut from being well-educated to not educated at all. Enterprising cooks took advantage of their talents and made themselves useful performing other tasks. Some cooks wrote letters to families and sweethearts for the cowboys who didn't know how to write. Other cooks had musical or storytelling talent, and still others could read or recite poetry and plays. Some cowboys used their talents for free, but others charged an extra fee for helping out.

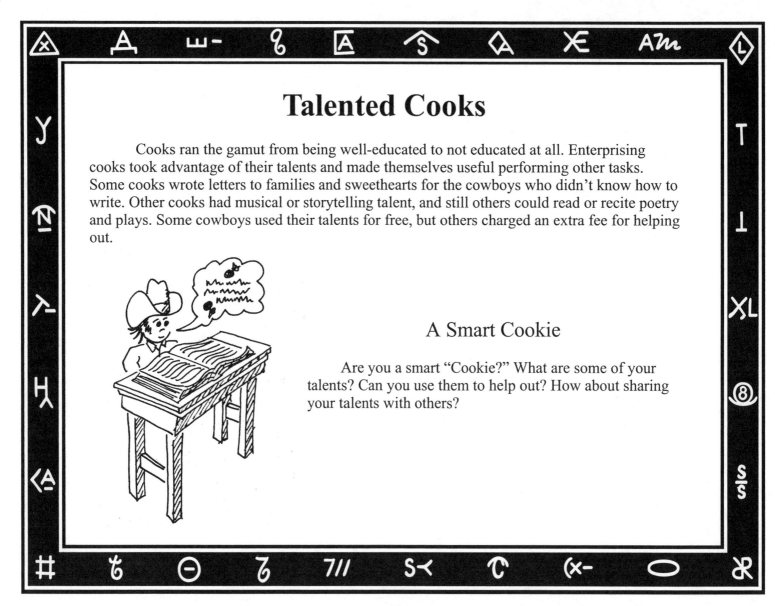

A Smart Cookie

Are you a smart "Cookie?" What are some of your talents? Can you use them to help out? How about sharing your talents with others?

Thongs for Fastening

A thong is a long strip of leather. Thongs, as fasteners, hold pieces of leather together by edge braiding and thong applique. They can be woven into fancy buttons. Thongs are used on belts, bridles, and quirts. Reins are often made from braided thongs.

Make Some Thongs

To make a thong, use a circular piece of rawhide. Begin by cutting a narrow slice around the outside and spiral toward the center. A thong can be as small as 3/32 of an inch. You can make yours wider. If you don't have a piece of rawhide, you can use straight strips from ultra suede, felt, or denim. Braid your thongs. Use them to gussy up your Sunday best clothing.

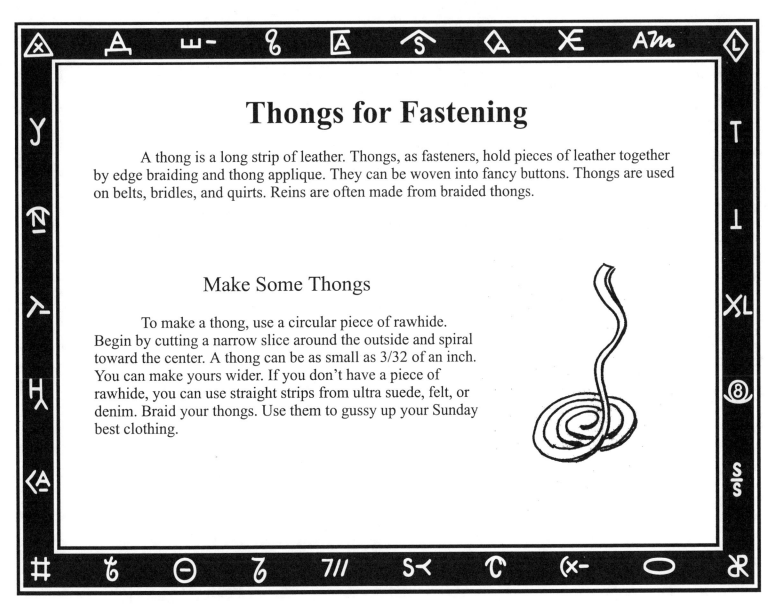

The Camp Cook

A "coosie" cooked outdoors most of the time. He served two to three meals a day, often in several different locations. The hours were long, beginning before daylight and finishing late at night, with little rest. He had to deal with shortages of supplies, bad weather conditions, and often did not know how many cowboys to cook for. Experienced cow camp cooks had little trouble finding jobs, because they were crucial to any cow camp. A good humored cook helped keep morale up. Overall, cooks were respected and well paid. Usually they made more money than the rest of the outfit, with the exception of the foreman or trail boss. No one messed with the cook.

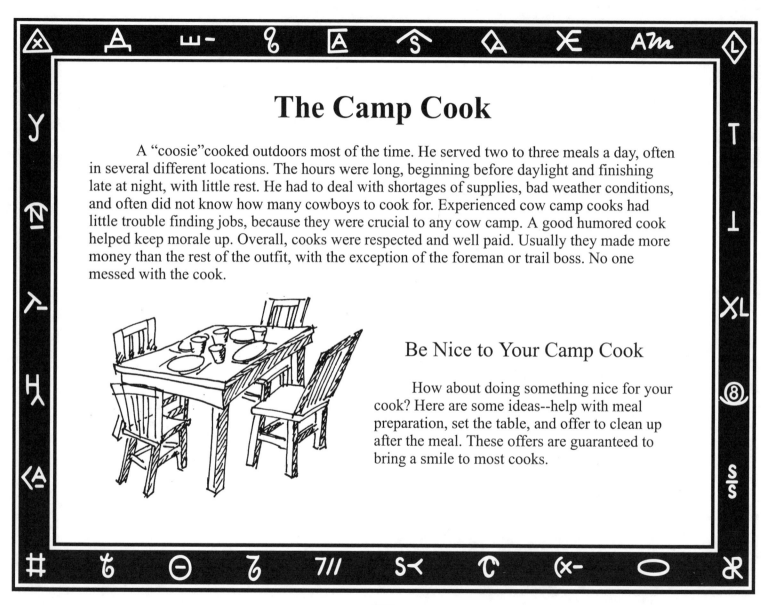

Be Nice to Your Camp Cook

How about doing something nice for your cook? Here are some ideas--help with meal preparation, set the table, and offer to clean up after the meal. These offers are guaranteed to bring a smile to most cooks.

Cowboy Weather Terms

Cowboys spend a great deal of their time outside. It seems reasonable that they have some terms for the harsh weather they deal with. Below are a few of their favorite ways of describing nature's conditions.

- ▶ Blue whistler = a strong wind
- ▶ Cow skinner = a severe winter storm
- ▶ Dust devil = a whirling cloud of dust
- ▶ Duster = a sandstorm
- ▶ Fence lifter = a heavy rain
- ▶ Gully washer = a hard rain
- ▶ Lay the dust = a light sprinkle of rain
- ▶ Sand auger = a small whirlwind
- ▶ Silver thaw = a rain that freezes as it touches the ground

Cowboy Weather Forecasting

Make some cowboy weather forecasts using some of the cowboy weather terms above.

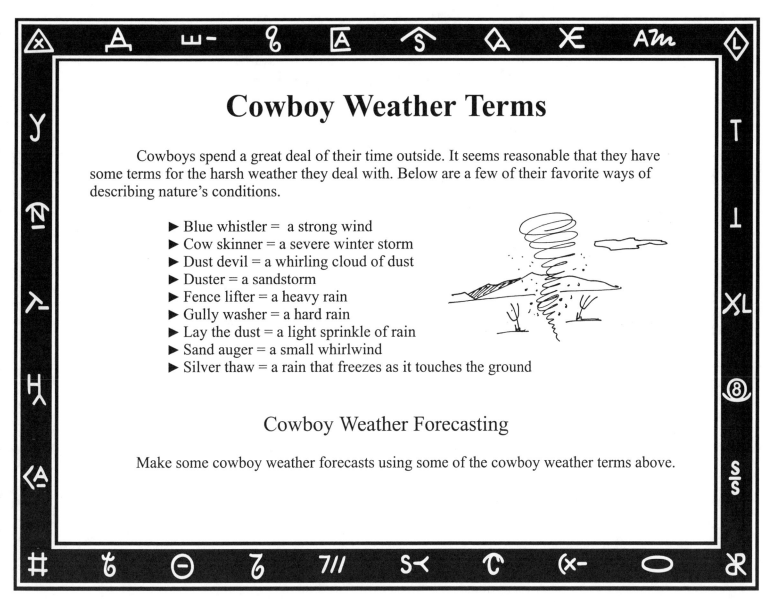

The Cowboy's Rope

There are several names for the rope a cowboy used. Cowboys from Mexico called it the Spanish word for rope, *"la riata."* American cowboys shortened it to "lariat." They also called it a "lasso," from the Spanish word "lazo." In the early days, cowboys made ropes from hides of animals, like the elk and the buffalo. Cowboys spent hours cutting strips from the hides and braiding the strips into ropes. Then they had to roll, pound, boil and grease the ropes to ready them for use.

Preparing a Rope for Use

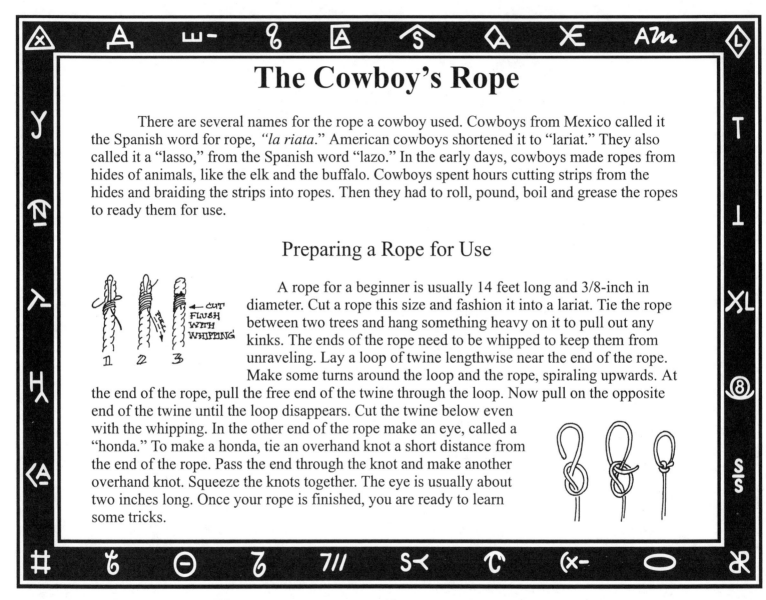

A rope for a beginner is usually 14 feet long and 3/8-inch in diameter. Cut a rope this size and fashion it into a lariat. Tie the rope between two trees and hang something heavy on it to pull out any kinks. The ends of the rope need to be whipped to keep them from unraveling. Lay a loop of twine lengthwise near the end of the rope. Make some turns around the loop and the rope, spiraling upwards. At the end of the rope, pull the free end of the twine through the loop. Now pull on the opposite end of the twine until the loop disappears. Cut the twine below even with the whipping. In the other end of the rope make an eye, called a "honda." To make a honda, tie an overhand knot a short distance from the end of the rope. Pass the end through the knot and make another overhand knot. Squeeze the knots together. The eye is usually about two inches long. Once your rope is finished, you are ready to learn some tricks.

Gittin' Ready Cowboy Style

The first thing a cowboy puts on at daybreak is his hat, then his shirt, trousers, socks and finally boots. At the end of the day, the cowboy reverses the process. He takes off his boots first, then his socks, next his trousers, shirt and last of all, his hat. The hat is set beside his bedroll with the boots set on the brim so it won't blow away in a nighttime breeze.

Dress and Undress Like a Cowboy

It's your turn to dress and undress like a cowboy. In the morning, start at the top and work down, and at nighttime, start at the bottom and work up.

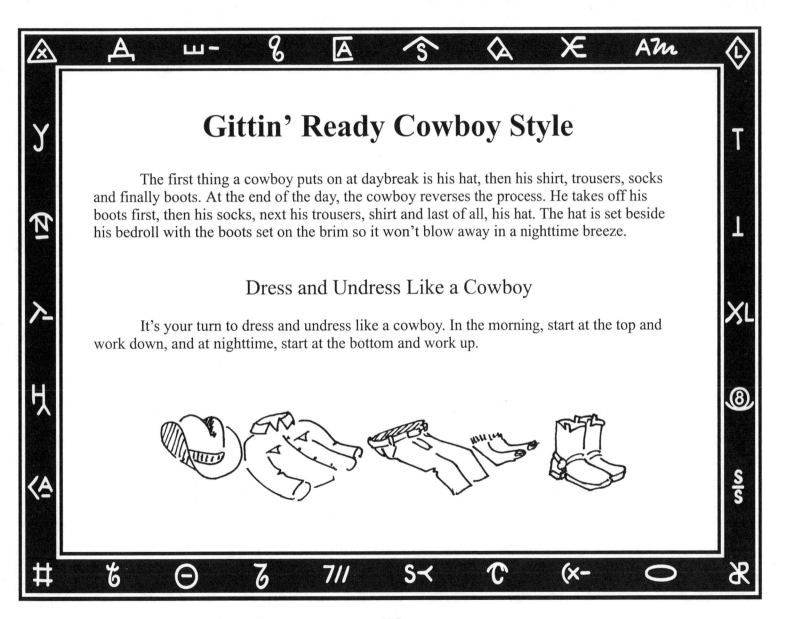

Camp Cook Cures All

There were few trained physicians in the Old West. While on the trail, the camp cooks took on the role of doctors. They relied on common sense and treated all kinds of illnesses, like colds, sore throats, snakebites, toothaches, diarrhea, and injuries.

Stir Up a Cowboy Cure

Here's a recipe for a sore throat:

> 2 tablespoons cider vinegar
> 2 tablespoons water
> 1 teaspoon salt
> Pinch of pepper

Next time you have a sore throat mix the ingredients together. Gargle every hour. If you try this, you're brave enough to fight a rattler and give him the first bite.

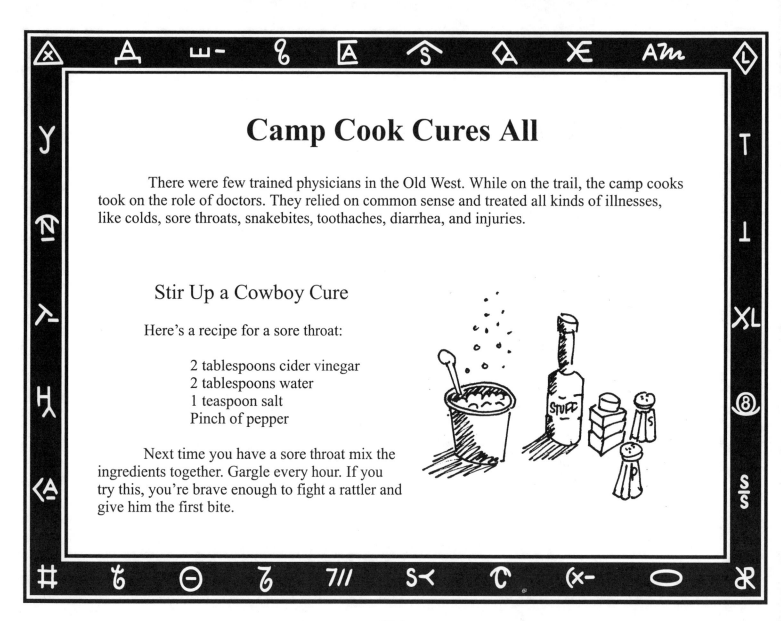

A Cowboy Takes Care of His Rope

If a rope was thrown down, it could become tangled or get kinked. A rope was an important tool for a cowboy and he never knew when he might need it in a hurry. He used it to tie up a horse, pull wagons across rivers or out of quicksand, haul wood, and throw cattle. When his rope was coiled, it would run out easily when thrown. A cowboy knew if he took care of his rope it would last about ten years, but if he didn't, it wouldn't last a season.

Coil a Rope

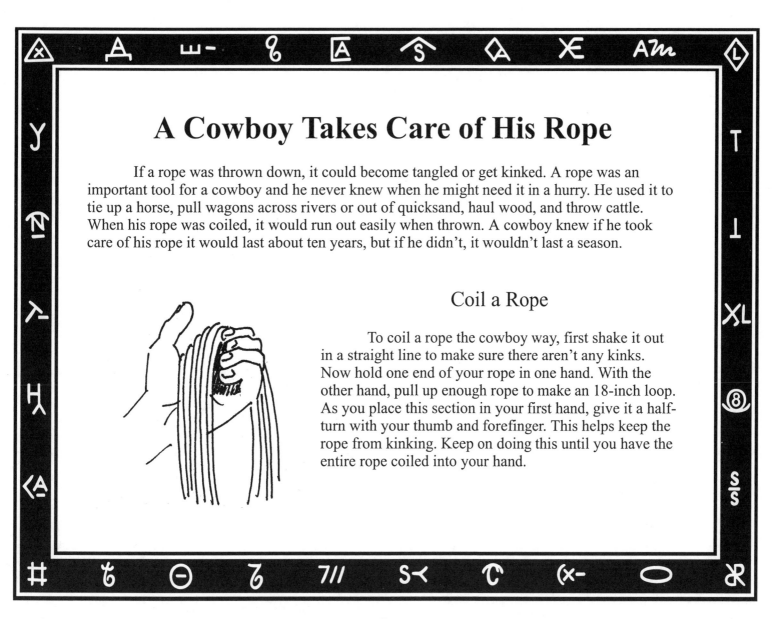

To coil a rope the cowboy way, first shake it out in a straight line to make sure there aren't any kinks. Now hold one end of your rope in one hand. With the other hand, pull up enough rope to make an 18-inch loop. As you place this section in your first hand, give it a half-turn with your thumb and forefinger. This helps keep the rope from kinking. Keep on doing this until you have the entire rope coiled into your hand.

The Pony Express

The Pony Express was a fast mail service that began April 3, 1860. Mail carriers hauled letters in a leather pouch, riding their horses day and night between St. Joseph, Missouri, and Sacramento, California, a distance of almost 2000 miles. It took from eight to ten days to make the trip. Existing stagecoach stations served as stops on the way, where a new rider and new horse took over. In March of 1861, a copy of President Lincoln's inaugural address was carried in record time, seven days and seven minutes. The Pony Express quit operating on October 26, 1861, because a faster means of communication was invented, the telegraph.

Make Deliveries by Way of the Pony Express

With some friends, set up some relief stations and run a Pony Express Relay. Post runners at the different stations and run the route, stopping only at stations to switch runners. Use a stop watch to keep track of your times. See how fast you can travel from the beginning to the end of your route. What's your record time?

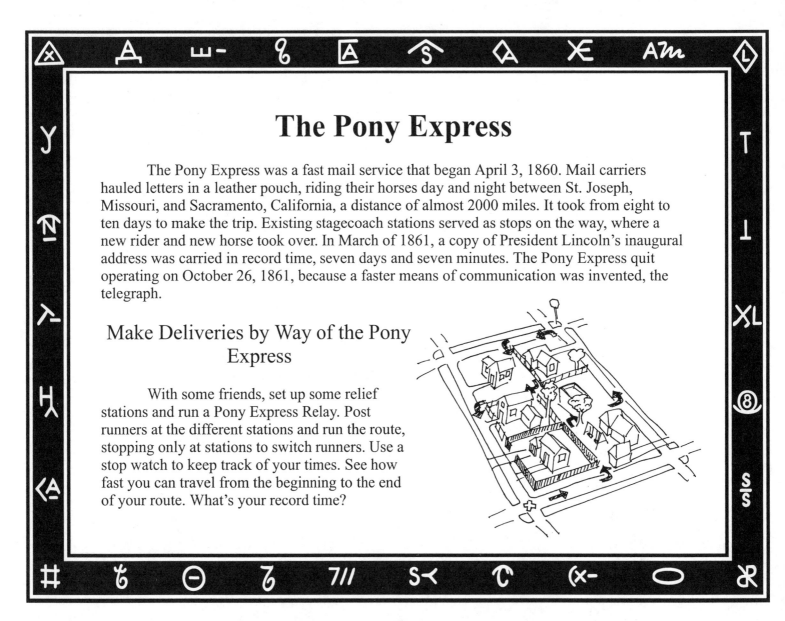

Sorghum Molasses

In the old days, cowboys were mighty familiar with sorghum molasses. Sorghum grows to about eight feet tall. It has a grain on the top and leaves on the stalk. Juice is squeezed out of the stalk and boiled into syrup. Cowboys spread it on biscuits and bread. It was so common that it had several nicknames, "lick" and "long sweetin." The reason it was so widespread is because it was the cheapest syrup money could buy. It was half the price of maple syrup and two thirds the price of cane sugar. If a camp ran out of "lick" an experienced "cookie" could mix up a substitute. He browned sugar in a skillet and added water.

Make Some Syrup

With your trail boss's help, make your own syrup. Pour ½ cup granulated sugar in a frying pan. Turn the burner to the medium setting. When you see the sugar start to melt, stir slowly. It will bubble and brown. Once it has melted, remove from heat and add ½ cup boiling water. For a different taste, add a little vanilla or orange flavoring. It gets darn hot, so have your trail boss pour the syrup on your biscuits or flapjacks.

Cowboys Snake Things Around

Snaking was a cowboy's favorite way of moving things from place to place. He tied things that were too heavy to carry, like logs, brush, and boulders, to the end of a rope. The other end of the rope was fastened around the horn of his saddle. Then he jumped on his horse and dragged the load behind him and his horse.

Snake Something Around

What item do you need to tote from one place to another? Use your lariat and tie it around your item. Drag it along behind you.

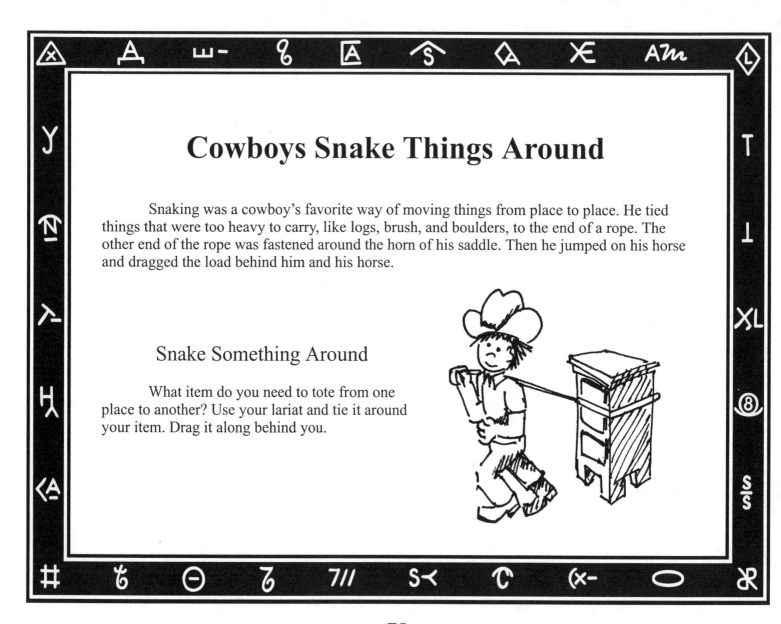

The Cookie

"Cookie" was a nickname for the camp cook. He was more than a cook because he performed other duties besides cooking, such as taking on the role of camp doctor, dentist, baker, barber, and sometimes helped with a stampeding herd. As a healer, he treated diarrhea, broken bones, and gunshot wounds. As the dentist he pulled teeth. He even cut hair and trimmed beards when necessary.

Take On Some New Camp Chores

So you're not a doctor, dentist or even a barber, but you probably have talents that will help in your camp. What are some other ways you can help out? Are there other chores you could start doing? Git a movin'.

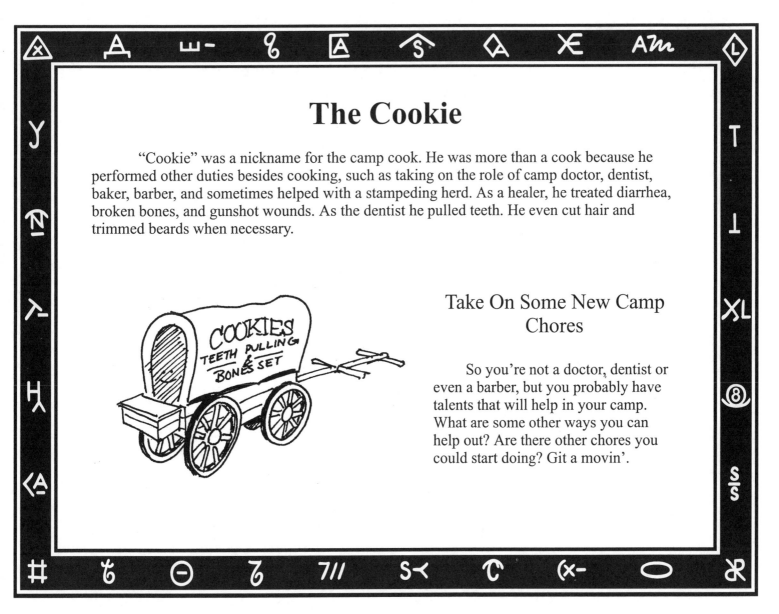

Many Kinds of Horses

Some cowboys liked solid-colored horses and others liked horses with distinctive markings, such as the appaloosas and the pintos. Appaloosas are spotted. Some have small white spots on a darker background, others are white with dark spots. There are other variations as well. Pintos are also called calico and paint horses. They are mostly white but have random patches of black or another dark color all over their bodies. They were favored by American Indians as a war horse, because their coloring gave a natural camouflage. Palominos are golden-tan or cream colored horses with white tails and manes. Bays have red-brown coats. They may be light, standard, mahogany or other shades of brown. They have black on the mane, tail, legs, and hooves.

Have a Horse Race

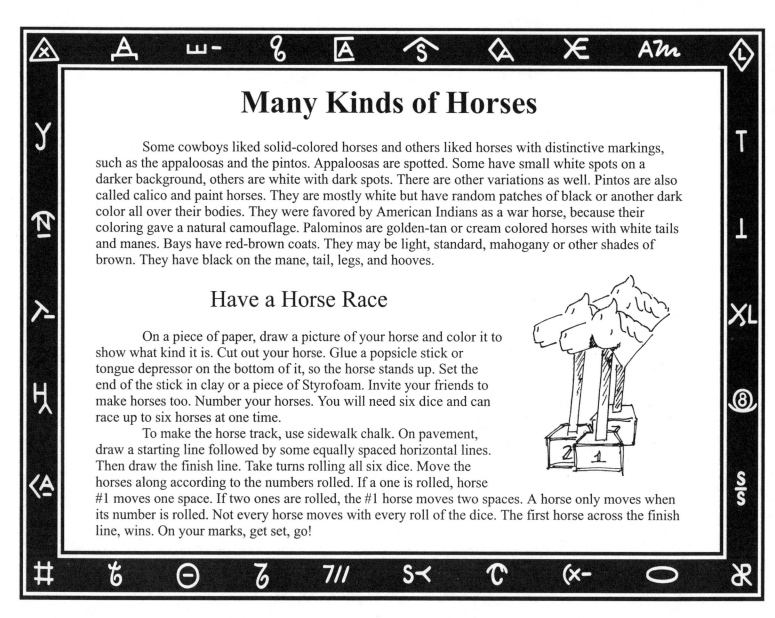

On a piece of paper, draw a picture of your horse and color it to show what kind it is. Cut out your horse. Glue a popsicle stick or tongue depressor on the bottom of it, so the horse stands up. Set the end of the stick in clay or a piece of Styrofoam. Invite your friends to make horses too. Number your horses. You will need six dice and can race up to six horses at one time.

To make the horse track, use sidewalk chalk. On pavement, draw a starting line followed by some equally spaced horizontal lines. Then draw the finish line. Take turns rolling all six dice. Move the horses along according to the numbers rolled. If a one is rolled, horse #1 moves one space. If two ones are rolled, the #1 horse moves two spaces. A horse only moves when its number is rolled. Not every horse moves with every roll of the dice. The first horse across the finish line, wins. On your marks, get set, go!

The Use of Rosettes

A rosette is a round piece of leather or metal with two slits in it. Long leather thongs are strung through the slits. It's used for ornamentation and for fastening things onto saddles. The rosettes, with the thongs, hold bridles together. They hold the brow band to the cheek straps, and provide a place to attach bits and bridle reins. Long thongs with some rosettes strung through them can help hold down articles that the cowboy carries on his saddle, such as blankets, ponchos, and slickers.

Make Some Rosettes

To make some rosettes, cut several flower-like shapes out of cardboard. Cover them with aluminum foil. Cut two parallel slits in the center of each one. String some leather bands or ribbons through them. Use the rosettes and some thongs to bundle up some clothing.

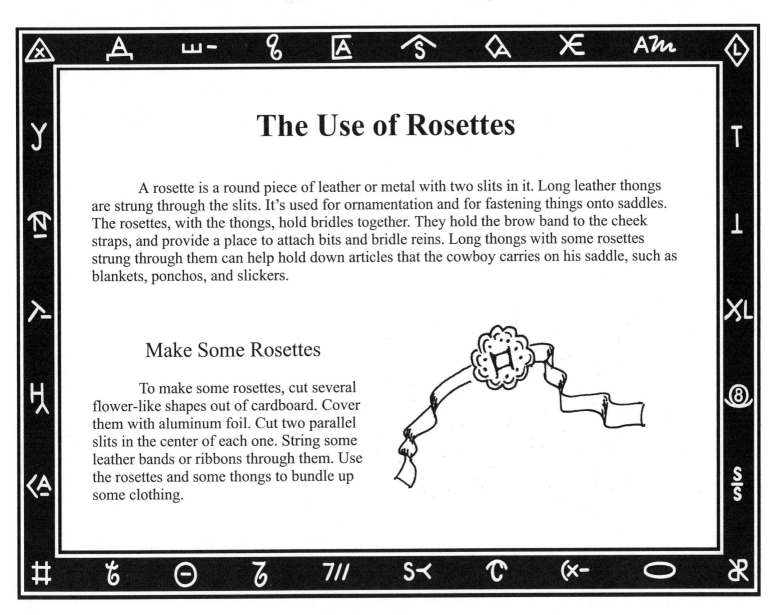

Cowboys Liked Spotted Pup

A dessert called "spotted pup" was popular in cowboy camps. It was boiled rice with raisins. If available, eggs, milk, and a little cinnamon would be added. Next time you have rice for dinner, ask your "coosie" to set aside two cups of rice for you or ask him to help you with the recipe below.

Ingredients:

1 cup water
1 cup instant rice
1 tablespoon butter or margarine
½ cup of raisins

In a pot, bring the water to a boil. Remove it from the heat. Pour in the instant rice and butter or margarine. Add the raisins. Mix the ingredients together. Cover the pot and let it stand for five minutes. Now scoop some into your bowl. Add a sprinkling of cinnamon if you wish. You could substitute milk for the water to make a creamier dessert.

Pole Fences

A pole fence was made without the vertical posts used in most fences. Instead, the ends of the beams rested one on top of another. Each section of wooden beams were set at an angle, forming a zig zag pattern. This pattern kept the fence from falling down.

Build a Pole Fence

Make your fence out of popsicle sticks. Set two sticks at an angle to each other, overlap them at the end. Put a little glue on top of one and set the other one on top of the glue. Zig zag a row of popsicle sticks overlapping and gluing as you go. Run another layer of sticks over the first layer, until it's as high as you want it.

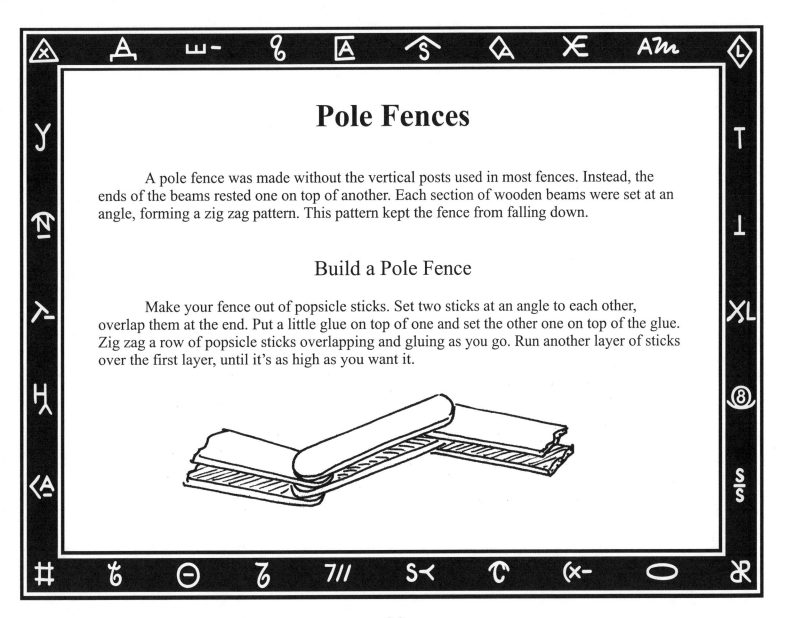

Ropes Made From Hemp

Some ropes that became popular with the cowboys were made from tough plant fibers called "hemp." The plants grown for their fiber come from various parts of the world. Manila hemp comes from the Philippines. Sisal fibers come from Africa, Brazil and Haiti. Henequen comes from the Yucatan in Mexico and Cuba. Still other hemp comes from Italy, Chile and Yugoslavia.

These new ropes made from hemp could be knotted to form a honda and were long enough to be "dallied," that is, wrapped around the saddle horn to hold a roped steer.

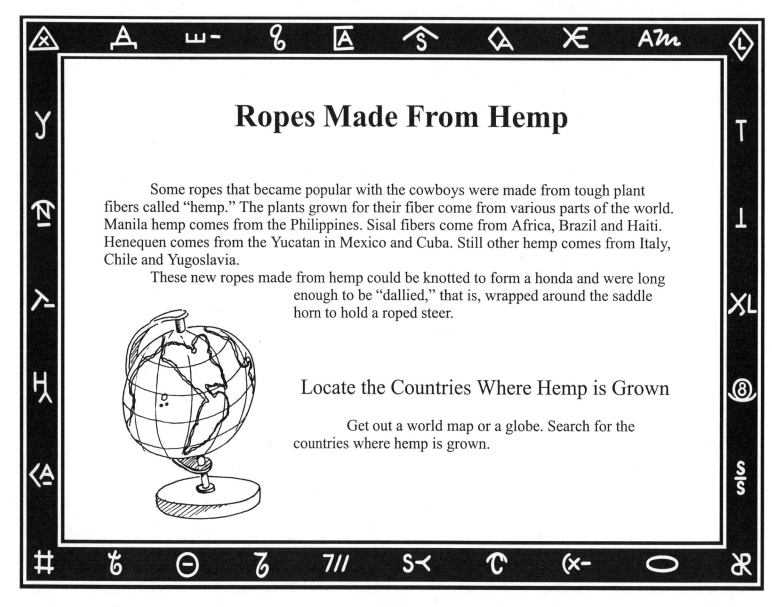

Locate the Countries Where Hemp is Grown

Get out a world map or a globe. Search for the countries where hemp is grown.

Cowboys Tell Windies

A "windy" is another name for a tall tale. For entertainment, cowboys told these boastful stories. They held no truth and the cowboys knew it. It was a competition as to who could tell the wildest tale. After telling his story, the cowboy would say, "Tie one onto that," which challenged the other cowboy to top his story and tell a wilder or funnier story.

Tell a Windy or Two

Make up your own funny tales and take turns telling them. Here's an example: "That steer wouldn't come outta that thicket fer nothin', so I sat myself down to eat some of the sorriest grub, I'd ever done cooked. That steer took one whiff of those sour beans and he came a runnin'. I dished him out some of them beans and he's been a followin' me 'round like a hound dog ever since. Now tie one onto that."

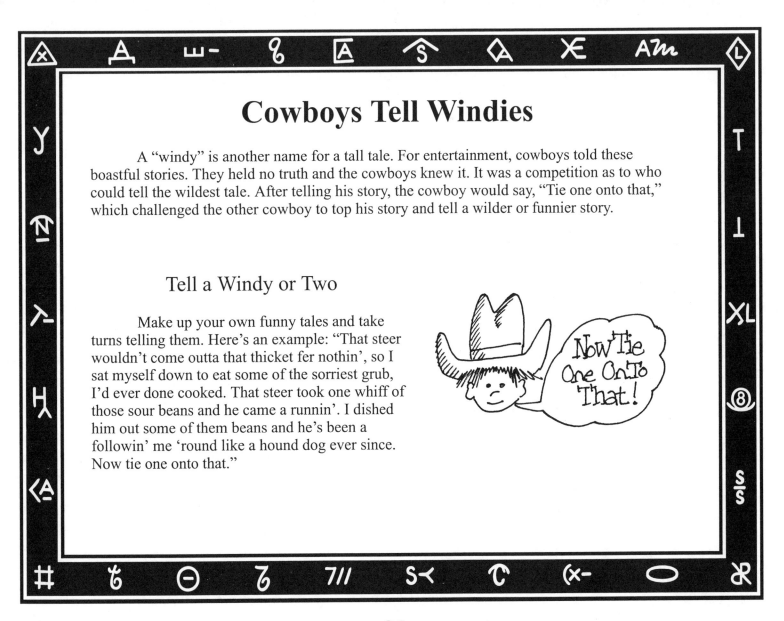

The Cowboy's Hat

Cowboys called their hats Stetsons, after the person that manufactured them. It was important to have a good hat, preferably a Stetson. The hat served as an umbrella when it rained. The brim shaded a cowboy's face when the sun beat down. Or he could use the hat to fan himself. It protected him from sleet and snow. He also used it to carry water to his horse, and a cowboy wouldn't think twice about throwing it at a charging bull. Wow! That's some hat.

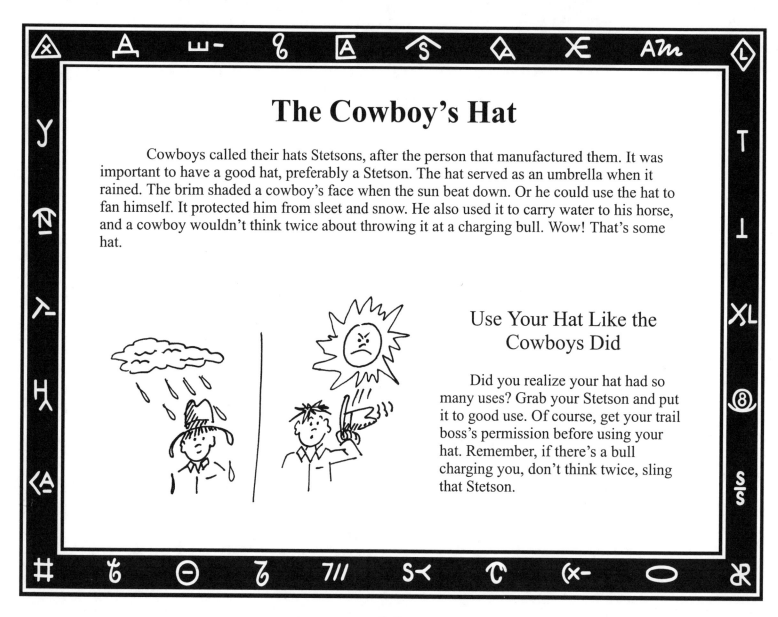

Use Your Hat Like the Cowboys Did

Did you realize your hat had so many uses? Grab your Stetson and put it to good use. Of course, get your trail boss's permission before using your hat. Remember, if there's a bull charging you, don't think twice, sling that Stetson.

Cowboys Tie Knots

A cowboy used his lariat when he branded calves or broke wild horses. He threw the rope around the animal and then wrapped the other end of the rope around a post to keep the rope taut. The clove hitch was good for fastening their lariats to a post.

Make a Clove Hitch

To make this knot, wrap your rope around a post, cross one end over the other to form an "x." Wrap the rope around the post a second time making another "x." Now pull the end up under the second "x." Tighten the knot by pulling on the end of the rope. Try it out by tying up your hoss or bicycle to a fence post.

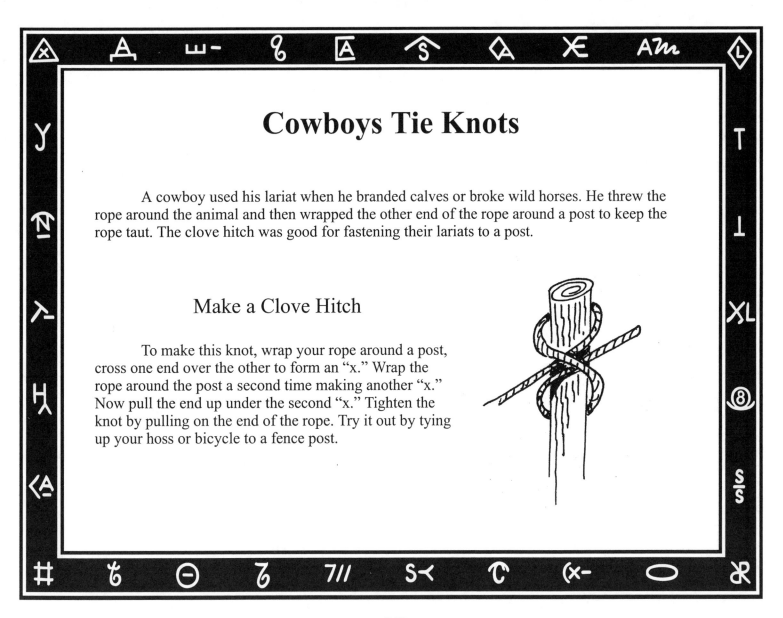

A Cowboy's Vest

Many cowboys wore leather, canvas, or wool vests over their shirts. A vest kept a cowboy warm on cold nights, but he also wore it for the pockets. Some cowboys collected items, such as buffalo teeth, gold nuggets, and arrowheads for good luck or to show friends. A cowboy couldn't use the pockets in his pants while sitting on a horse, so he stored personal belongings in his vest pockets.

Make a Cowboy Vest

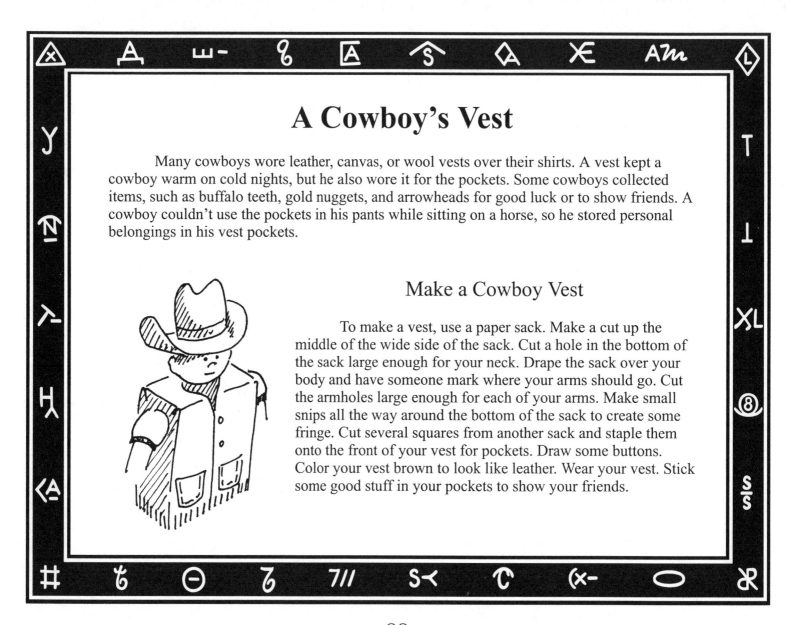

To make a vest, use a paper sack. Make a cut up the middle of the wide side of the sack. Cut a hole in the bottom of the sack large enough for your neck. Drape the sack over your body and have someone mark where your arms should go. Cut the armholes large enough for each of your arms. Make small snips all the way around the bottom of the sack to create some fringe. Cut several squares from another sack and staple them onto the front of your vest for pockets. Draw some buttons. Color your vest brown to look like leather. Wear your vest. Stick some good stuff in your pockets to show your friends.

Cowboy Geography

Cowboys sometimes had to give directions to other cowboys. They might need to point out another section of the range or how to get to a pretty girl's home. When this happened, they would grab a stick, their version of a pen, and scratch out a map in the dirt. A cowboy could talk better with a stick in his hand.

Do Some Cowboy Geography

Grab yourself a stick and find some dirt, now give a cowboy friend directions. Scratch out the landmarks in your area and then draw a route to get the cowboy where he wants to go.

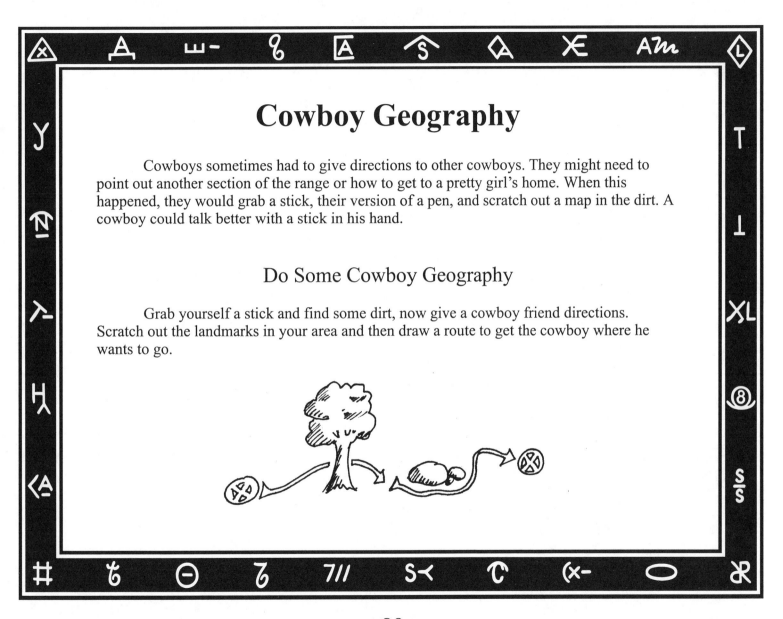

Cowboys Play Crack-A-Loo

Crack-a-loo was a game that cowboys played using coins. A cowboy would pick out a special landmark in a room, such as a crack in the floor. Then he would pitch a coin against the ceiling of the room and watch it fall to the floor. Each cowboy got a turn. Whoever came nearest to the crack would win the game.

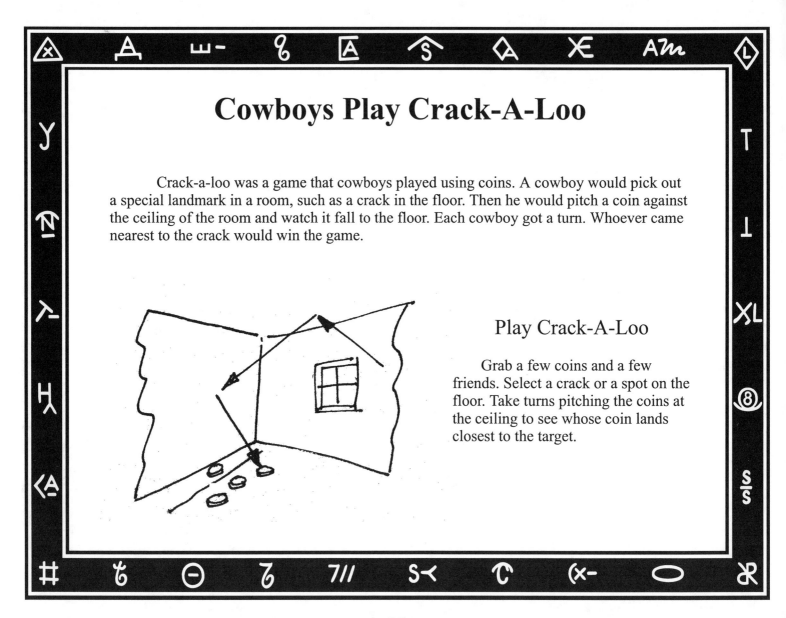

Play Crack-A-Loo

Grab a few coins and a few friends. Select a crack or a spot on the floor. Take turns pitching the coins at the ceiling to see whose coin lands closest to the target.

Cowboys Braid

Braiding played an important roll in the Old West. Some cowboys were good at leatherwork. They braided belts, hackamores, bridles, reins, reatas, and quirts (a short-handled whip) using rawhide or horsehair. Horsehair ropes were too light to throw and they kinked too, but they worked well to tie up their horses and served as bridles. Sometimes cowboys braided miniature lariats using hair from their favorite horse's tail. They used these miniature lariats as watch chains, good luck charms against snake strikes, or gave them to their special womenfolk.

Try Your Hand at Braiding

Make yourself a belt using the three thong flat braid or "hair braid." Cut three pieces of leather or macrame yarn to length, approximately 3 feet to 4 feet, depending on your waist and the type of material you use. If you use leather, rub it with saddle soap to make the strands easier to work. Place a piece of masking tape on each

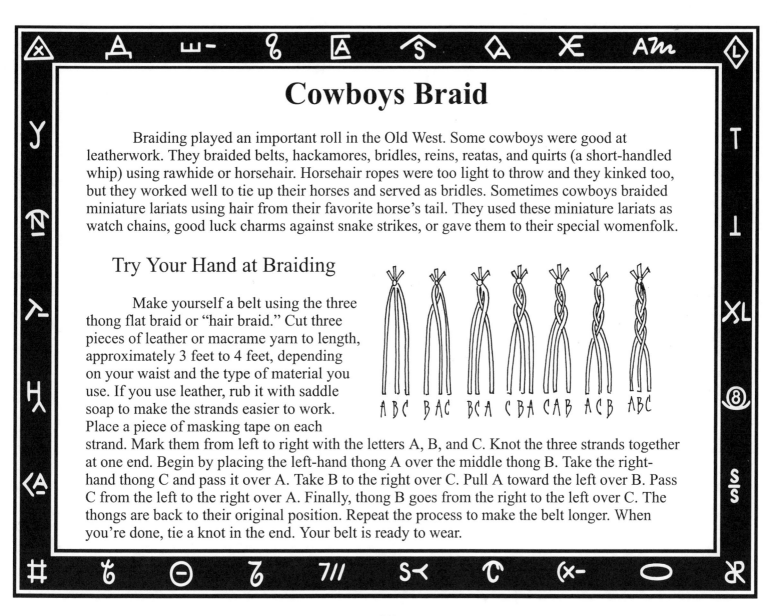

strand. Mark them from left to right with the letters A, B, and C. Knot the three strands together at one end. Begin by placing the left-hand thong A over the middle thong B. Take the right-hand thong C and pass it over A. Take B to the right over C. Pull A toward the left over B. Pass C from the left to the right over A. Finally, thong B goes from the right to the left over C. The thongs are back to their original position. Repeat the process to make the belt longer. When you're done, tie a knot in the end. Your belt is ready to wear.

A Cowboy's Breakfast

Cowboys added colorful phrases to our language. Some of the words they used described the foods they ate. A cowboy who woke up mighty hungry wanted a belly-filling breakfast. Here are a few of the items he might order--chuck wagon chicken (fried bacon), dough gods (biscuits), with some cow grease (butter). Then a cowboy might wash his food down with some belly-wash (weak coffee).

Order Breakfast Like a Cowboy

Order up your own cowboy breakfast. Of course, if you're a young cowboy or cowgirl, you might just pass on that belly-wash and order up some cow juice instead.

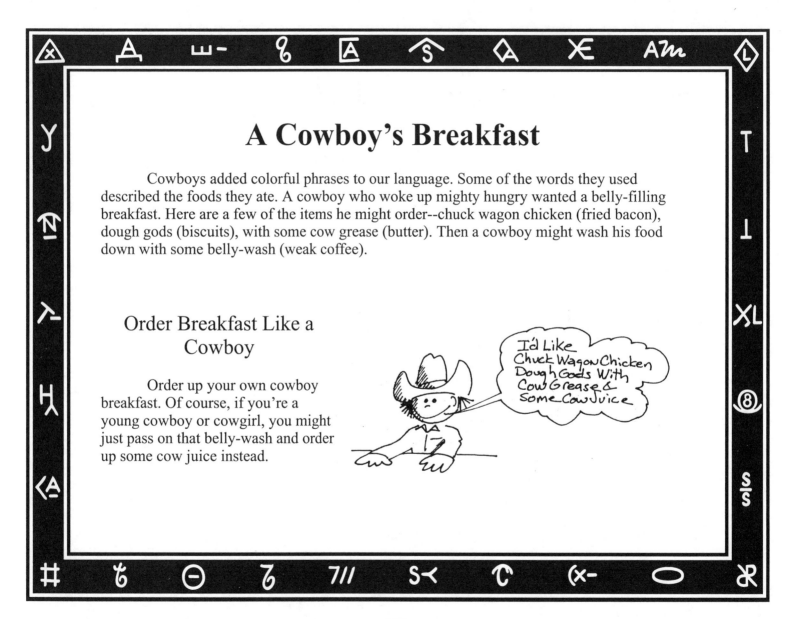

92

Stampeding Cattle

Git out of the way! It's a stampede! Cattle often stampeded on stormy nights, because they became spooked by the thunder and lightning. Actually, it's been said that there are a thousand reasons why cattle might stampede. Once cattle panicked, it was hard to calm them down again. Bringing them under control was a dangerous job for the cowboys. The cattle could become injured too. Cattle stampeded until they were exhausted. Sometimes cattle remained nervous for days after a stampede.

Stampede Like the Cattle

Get some friends together. Grab some pots, pans, and cookie sheets. Some of you bang the kitchen utensils to make storm noises. Others can be cattle that moo and bellow and stampede.

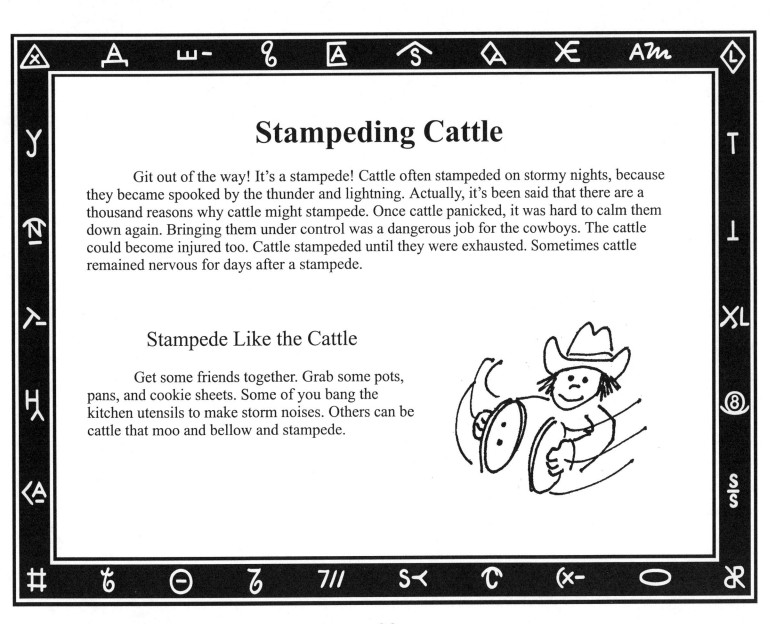

A Cowboy's Poke Pouch

A poke pouch was a small leather sack used to carry odds and ends and some personal articles, such as money, letters, and cards. The cowboy attached it to his belt with a piece of rawhide or stored it in his saddle bag.

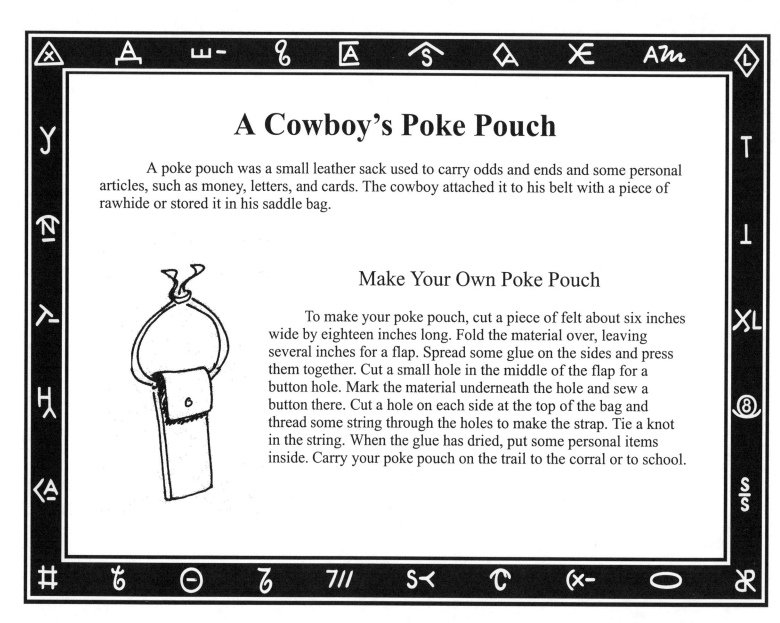

Make Your Own Poke Pouch

To make your poke pouch, cut a piece of felt about six inches wide by eighteen inches long. Fold the material over, leaving several inches for a flap. Spread some glue on the sides and press them together. Cut a small hole in the middle of the flap for a button hole. Mark the material underneath the hole and sew a button there. Cut a hole on each side at the top of the bag and thread some string through the holes to make the strap. Tie a knot in the string. When the glue has dried, put some personal items inside. Carry your poke pouch on the trail to the corral or to school.

A "Bowl of Red"

Camp cooks came from various ethnic backgrounds and nationalities. For example, there were Black, Mexican, German, and Scottish cooks that brought some specialty cooking to their cow camps. One of the dishes a Mexican camp cook prepared was chile con carne. This spicy Mexican dish was popular with the cowboys. It used ingredients they had readily available--beef and chiles. The recipe goes something like this:

2 pounds stew meat
1-14 ½ ounce can diced tomatoes
1- 4 ounce can green chile peppers
2 tablespoons lard or bacon drippings
1 onion
2 cloves of garlic

With adult help, chop the onion. Fry the chopped onion and garlic in the lard or bacon drippings. Add the chopped stew meat. Some sources say the best chili con carne was made using the eye of a bull. Now that's a cowboy challenge! Fry the meat with the garlic and onions. Dump the can of tomatoes and can of green chile peppers into the pan. Simmer on low for about twenty minutes. For a spicier concoction, use jalapeño chiles. Serve the chile con carne with frijoles, beans, and tortillas. Watch out for the cowboy winds that follow!

Keeping Peace in the Cow Towns

After months on the trail with their cattle, the cowboys were sure to have had troubles. They may have encountered various natural and manmade hazards, such as lack of water, getting bogged down in quicksand, high rivers to cross, stampedes, quarantines, cattle rustlers, and hostile Indians. It should come as no surprise that once the cowboys finally reached the cow towns, they were ready to be wild. In addition to rowdy cowboys, the towns also attracted other rough characters. These fairly new towns had no one to keep peace, until citizens got together and made rules. Then they hired marshals, sheriffs, and other peace officers to enforce the laws.

Make a Sheriff's Badge

To make a badge, draw two triangles having equal sides. Cut them out. Lay one triangle upside down on top of the other one, so that there are six points. Glue them together. Cover your star with aluminum foil. Glue or tape a large safety pin on the back. Now put it on. Congratulations, you've just been sworn in as the new sheriff in town. Go find a friend to be the deputy.

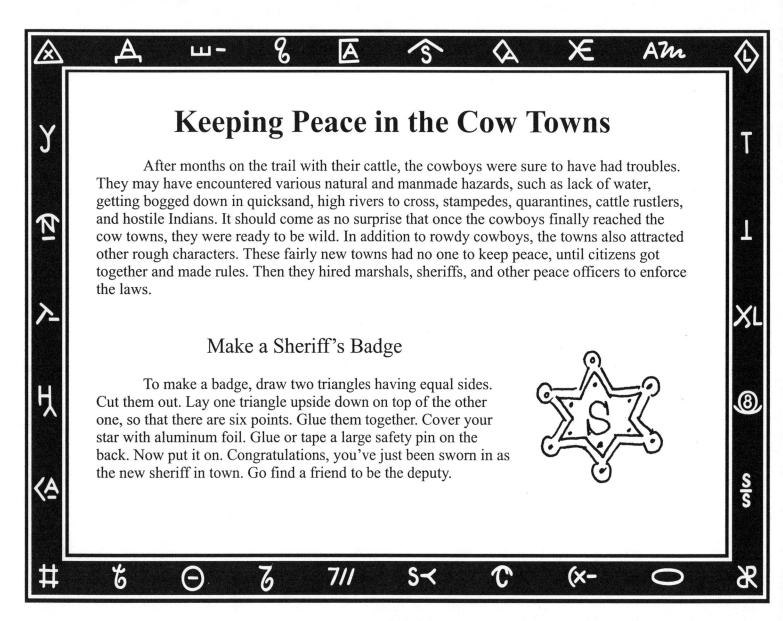

Cowboys Work in the Heat of the Day

Cowboys worked outside all day, even when the sun was blistering hot. Although a cowboy wore a hat to shade his head, he still had to be careful not to get too much sun. If a cowboy got too much sun, he could count on his "Coosie" to have a cure to treat him. But this cure would make any cowboy be very careful not to get overheated.

Try the Coosie's Cure for Heatstroke

Like a careful cowboy, protect your head from the hot sun and drink plenty of water. But if you do get a little too much heat, here's what to do. Wet a cloth and wrap it over your head. Wet a second cloth and fold it several times. Cover the cloth with salt and put it on your neck. Next, spread mustard on the calves of your legs and on the soles of your feet. Now that should cool you down and make you stink to high heaven. If you try this, you're as easy to convince as a hoss-fly in a mule's ear.

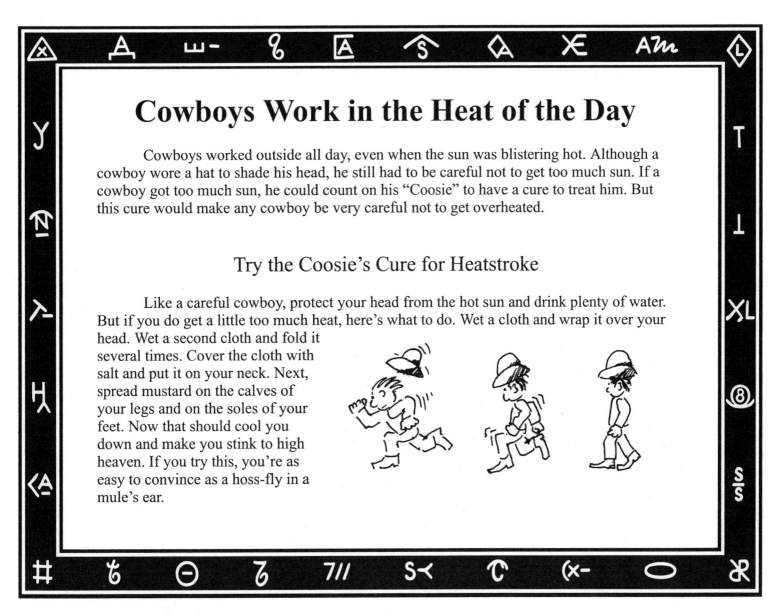

Cowboys Search for Water

Cowboys out on the trail or on a range sometimes ran out of water and had to search for some. In desperation they had to drink from rivers, pits, or any mud holes they could find. A cowboy could become very ill from drinking bad water. Sometimes they tried to clean the water by filtering it through rocks and sand before drinking it.

Clean Up Some Muddy Water

Here's one way to make muddy water a sight better lookin'. Punch some holes in the bottom of a bucket. Set some clean gravel over the holes. Above the gravel, pour lots of sand. Set the tub in a mud puddle, leaving a few inches of the tub above the water level. The water will filter in through the holes, gravel and sand. Water treated this way may not be pure enough to drink, but you could water plants with it.

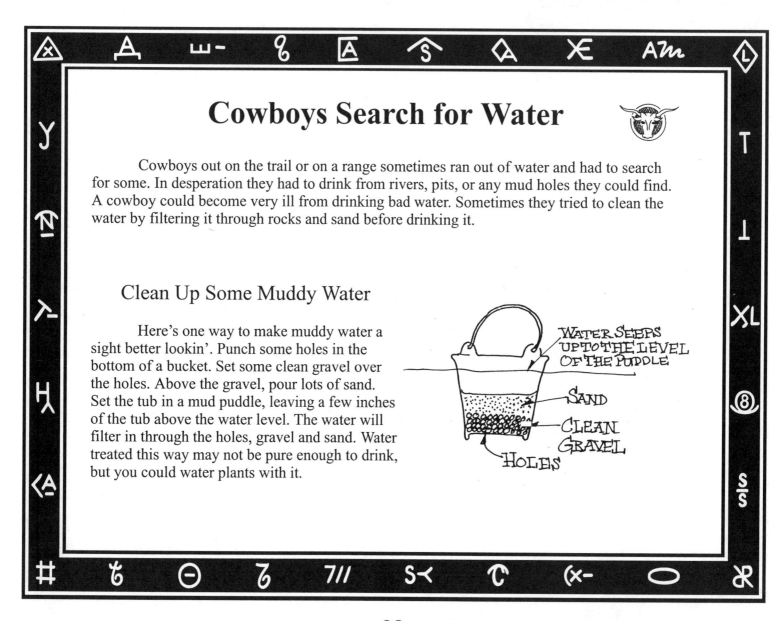

WATER SEEPS UP TO THE LEVEL OF THE PUDDLE

SAND

CLEAN GRAVEL

HOLES

"You're Makin' a Hand"

You're "makin' a hand, Pardner," was a way of praising a cowboy for being competent at his job and about being respectful to others. Most cowboys were upstanding dudes that lived by a code. They believed in courage, loyalty, cheerfulness, and laughing at hardships. If someone says to you, "you're makin' a hand," he is paying you a high compliment.

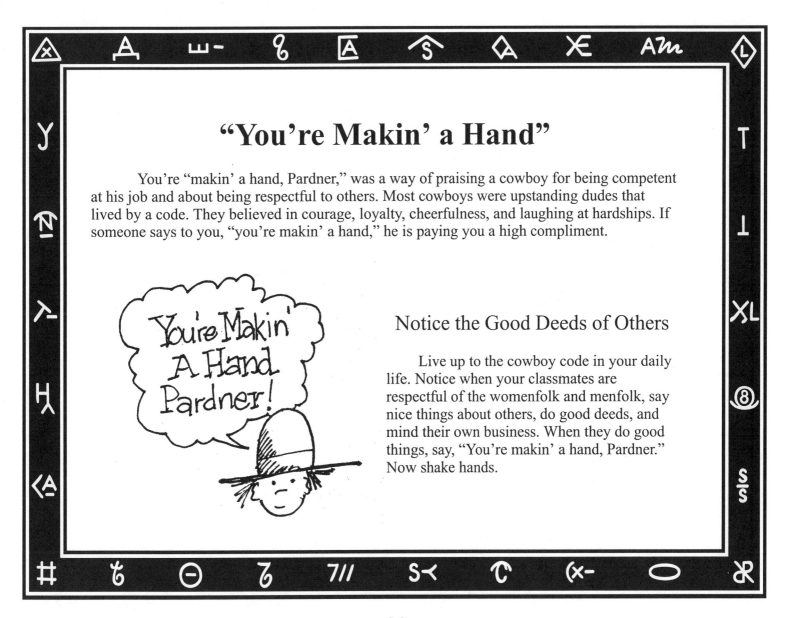

Notice the Good Deeds of Others

Live up to the cowboy code in your daily life. Notice when your classmates are respectful of the womenfolk and menfolk, say nice things about others, do good deeds, and mind their own business. When they do good things, say, "You're makin' a hand, Pardner." Now shake hands.

Cowboys Used Wild Horses

Early cowboys used wild "mustangs" as their work horses. They were small, but alert, quick, and had good "cow sense." The horses helped round up cattle, cut or separate cattle for branding, and rode herds. Extra horses were kept together in a "remuda." Each cowboy had six to twelve horses assigned to him. When one horse tired or a cowboy needed a horse with a special skill, he called for the wrangler, who was in charge of the extra horses, to bring him another horse from the remuda.

Make a Mustang

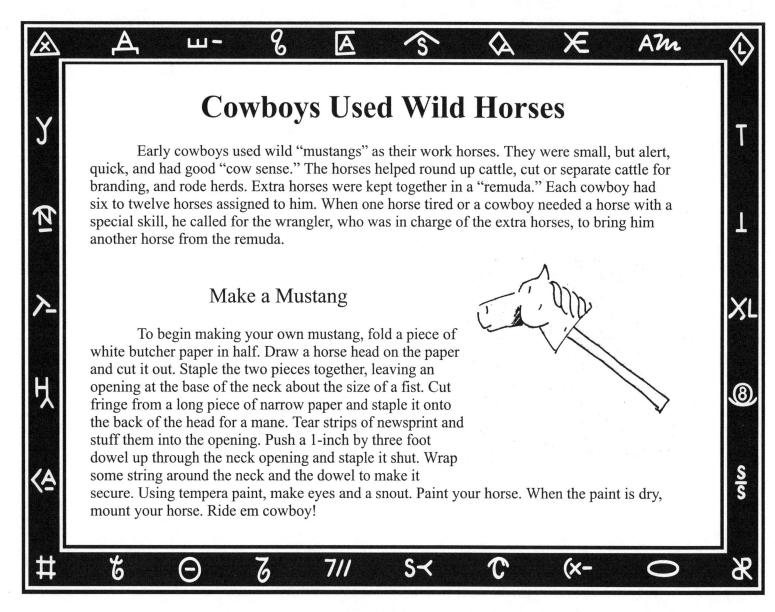

To begin making your own mustang, fold a piece of white butcher paper in half. Draw a horse head on the paper and cut it out. Staple the two pieces together, leaving an opening at the base of the neck about the size of a fist. Cut fringe from a long piece of narrow paper and staple it onto the back of the head for a mane. Tear strips of newsprint and stuff them into the opening. Push a 1-inch by three foot dowel up through the neck opening and staple it shut. Wrap some string around the neck and the dowel to make it secure. Using tempera paint, make eyes and a snout. Paint your horse. When the paint is dry, mount your horse. Ride em cowboy!

Man at the Pot

While on the trail, the cowboy's social life revolved around the campfire. That's where they talked, sang, told stories, ate, and drank their beloved coffee. It was only polite, if a cowboy got up to get a refill of his coffee and heard someone yell, "Man at the pot!" he was duty-bound by camp etiquette to make the rounds and fill all the cups held out to him.

Follow Cow Camp Etiquette

Next time you get up from the table to get a second serving of food or drink and you hear, "Man at the pot!" be sure you follow cow camp etiquette and offer to bring seconds for everyone at your dinner table.

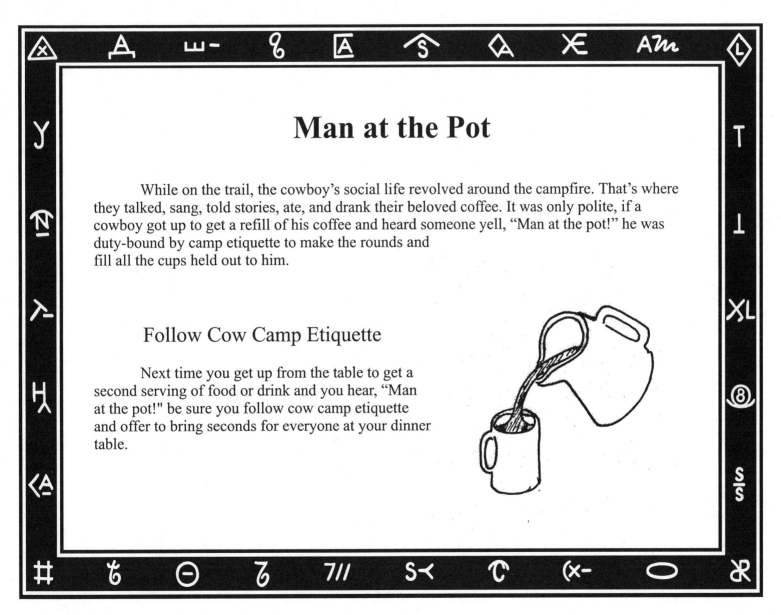

Old-Time Mercantiles

The mercantile of the old days carried a wide variety of well-selected stock to help folks survive in the West. Some of the items they stocked included clothing, underwear, household goods, boots, shoes, groceries, hardware, cutlery, and tools. Ranch folks traveled great distances and over rough terrain to buy the supplies they needed. Sometimes they bought a month's supply of merchandise at one time.

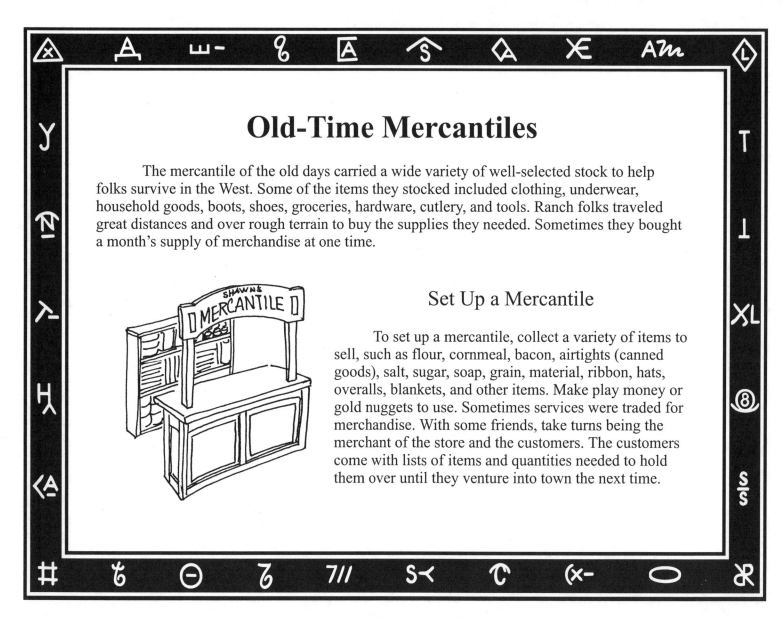

Set Up a Mercantile

To set up a mercantile, collect a variety of items to sell, such as flour, cornmeal, bacon, airtights (canned goods), salt, sugar, soap, grain, material, ribbon, hats, overalls, blankets, and other items. Make play money or gold nuggets to use. Sometimes services were traded for merchandise. With some friends, take turns being the merchant of the store and the customers. The customers come with lists of items and quantities needed to hold them over until they venture into town the next time.

Moccasin Mail

Trappers were the first to leave messages on trails. When parties of trappers used the same trail, the leading party often left a message to the following party. Messages warned of pitfalls or suggested safe routes. These messages were left in moccasins tied in tree branches. Later, cowboys on trails took to using this method of communicating with other cowboys. They would leave messages in the sand or in trees.

Leave Some Moccasin Mail

What message do you need to tell a friend or family member? Select a special place on a route you take and leave messages in the sand or use an old shoe or sock to hang from a tree. Leave a message in it. Maybe you want to tell other cowboys about hazards on the trail or cow rustlers you encountered.

Cowboys Complained About Their Bread

How would you describe hard, heavy bread? It's been said, "A cow camp cook can turn a 25-pound bag of flour into a ton of bread." Sometimes the bread or biscuits that cooks made turned out heavy. The cowboys eating the stuff came up with descriptions for the hard, heavy bread. Here are examples of their comments:

The bread was

- ▶ as heavy as lead.
- ▶ as solid as a rock.
- ▶ so stale the wolves wouldn't go near it.
- ▶ so hard a cowboy had to break it with an ax.

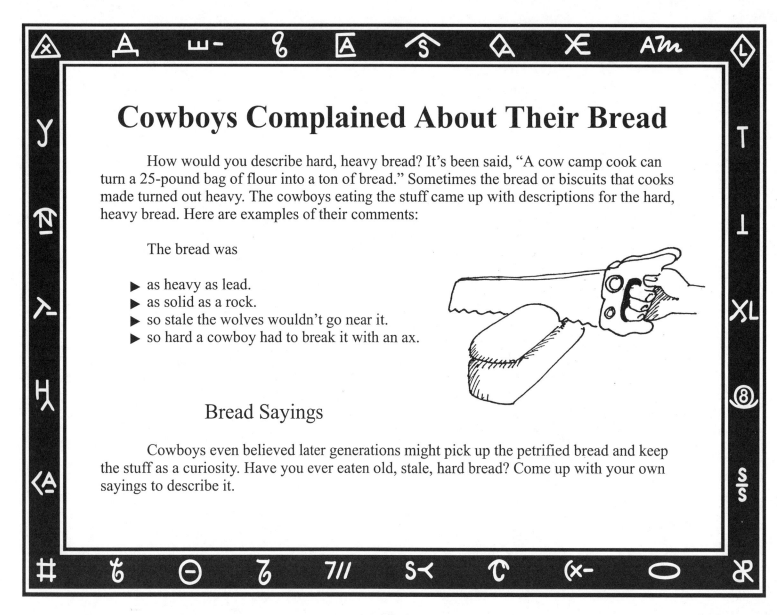

Bread Sayings

Cowboys even believed later generations might pick up the petrified bread and keep the stuff as a curiosity. Have you ever eaten old, stale, hard bread? Come up with your own sayings to describe it.

The Art of Spinning a Rope

Spinning a rope wasn't just for lassoing cattle, it was entertainment as well. It's believed that trick and fancy roping was brought into the United States years ago by Vincenti Orespo from Mexico. He worked with the Buffalo Bill Show where he was a whiz at roping horses. Others, such as Will Rogers, also performed as comedians and trick ropers.

Try Your Hand at Spinning a Rope

Ropes used for spinning are between 15 and 20 feet long. You need a rope that works well, # 12 solid-braided cotton sashcord, which is three-eighths inch thick, can be purchased in hardware stores. Prepare your rope for use (see page 72). To learn rope spinning you need to start with the simplest form, that of making flat, horizontal loops. Begin by standing with your feet slightly apart. Bend forward at the waist. Keep your arms below your waist. Start with a small loop, about two feet in diameter. Pull the rope through your hand, until you take up the slack, but leave at least a foot of rope between your hands and the loop. Start twirling the rope slowly. The trick to spinning a rope is rhythm, not speed. Once you master that, jump in and out of the loop. Can you twirl the loop high into the air?

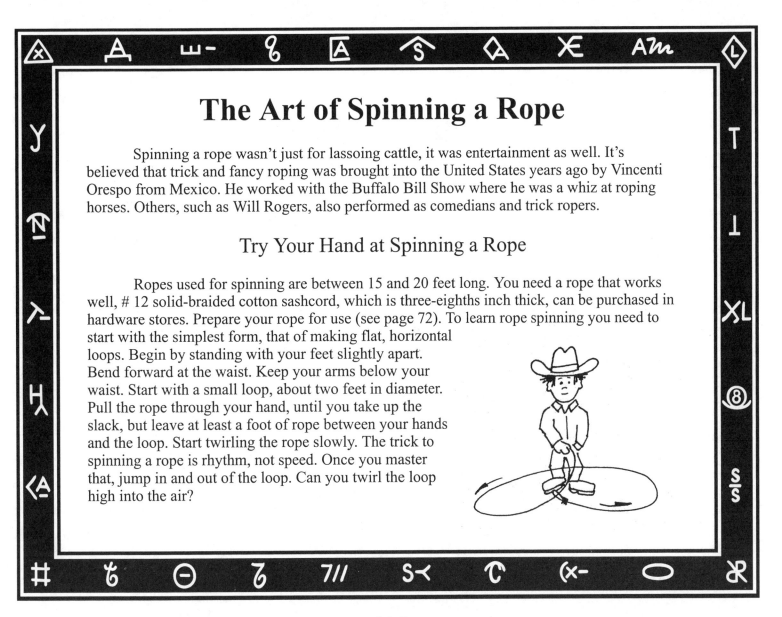

Cowboy Superstitions

A superstition is a belief that an action or event causes an unrelated event to happen. Many cowboys were superstitious. It was probably their rough, tough lifestyle full of hardships, diseases, injuries, and death that brought about so many superstitions. They didn't button their vests, because they believed a buttoned vest would trap a cold or rheumatism. Changing underwear was considered bad luck. If a cowboy slept in a bed, he never put his hat on it.

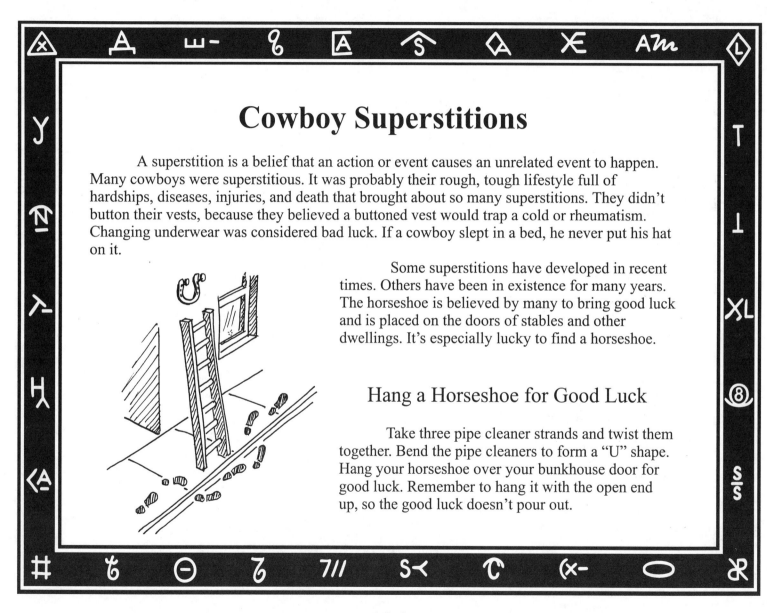

Some superstitions have developed in recent times. Others have been in existence for many years. The horseshoe is believed by many to bring good luck and is placed on the doors of stables and other dwellings. It's especially lucky to find a horseshoe.

Hang a Horseshoe for Good Luck

Take three pipe cleaner strands and twist them together. Bend the pipe cleaners to form a "U" shape. Hang your horseshoe over your bunkhouse door for good luck. Remember to hang it with the open end up, so the good luck doesn't pour out.

Cowboys Count Cattle

Ranchers sometimes needed to count their cattle, without herding them all together. If a rancher heard about cattle rustling in the area he might want to make sure none of his cattle were missing. Or if a rancher needed a loan, the banker would want to know that the rancher had something of worth, such as his cattle. The banker might want more than an estimate of the number of cattle, he might ask for a count. The rancher would send cowboys into the pastures to take a tally. One cowboy on horseback took the tally. The other cowboys moved the cattle past the counter.

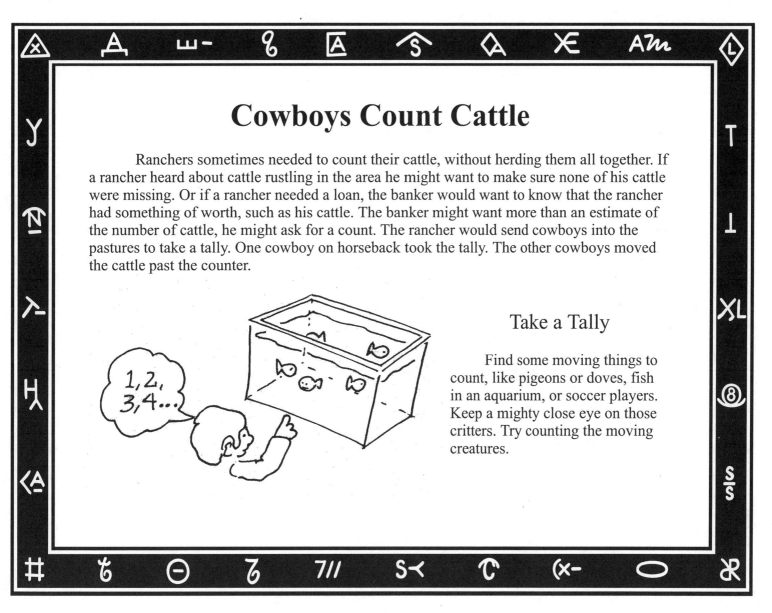

Take a Tally

Find some moving things to count, like pigeons or doves, fish in an aquarium, or soccer players. Keep a mighty close eye on those critters. Try counting the moving creatures.

The Family Brand

Some ranches had more than one brand, two different ones for the cattle and one for the horses. But most small ranches had one registered brand for the entire family. But what if the rancher had children? Instead of having a different brand for each member of a family, he added to the existing brand. For example, if the family brand was DD, the first child's brand would be DD 1, the second, DD 2, and so on.

Make a Brand for Your Family

Make up a family brand and add numbers behind it for the number of children in your family.

Flapjacks for Breakfast

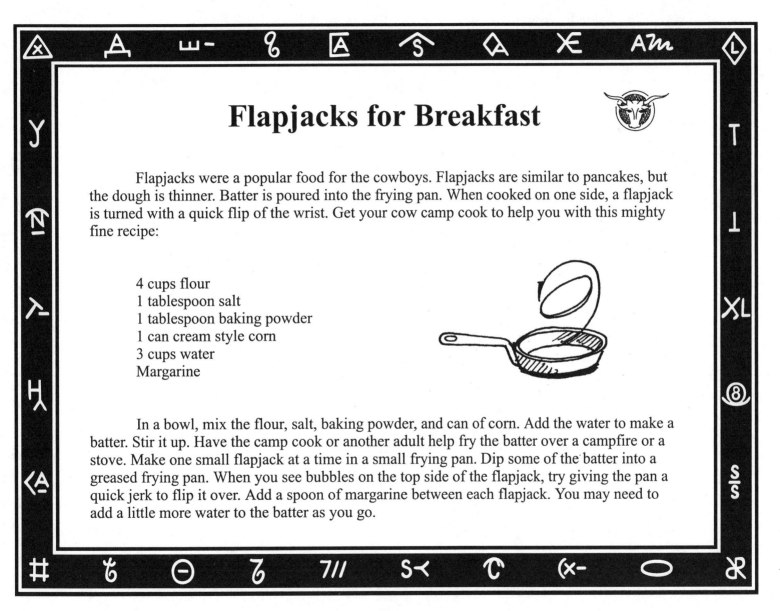

Flapjacks were a popular food for the cowboys. Flapjacks are similar to pancakes, but the dough is thinner. Batter is poured into the frying pan. When cooked on one side, a flapjack is turned with a quick flip of the wrist. Get your cow camp cook to help you with this mighty fine recipe:

4 cups flour
1 tablespoon salt
1 tablespoon baking powder
1 can cream style corn
3 cups water
Margarine

In a bowl, mix the flour, salt, baking powder, and can of corn. Add the water to make a batter. Stir it up. Have the camp cook or another adult help fry the batter over a campfire or a stove. Make one small flapjack at a time in a small frying pan. Dip some of the batter into a greased frying pan. When you see bubbles on the top side of the flapjack, try giving the pan a quick jerk to flip it over. Add a spoon of margarine between each flapjack. You may need to add a little more water to the batter as you go.

A Cowboy's Seasons

Cowboys had various ways of describing the different seasons. Some examples are:

"Between hay and grass" meant between winter and spring, when the hay was gone and the grass had not sprung up yet.

"Calf time" occurred in the spring.

"Coming grass" was the approaching spring.

"Fire season" was in the summer when the sun dried out the grasses and fires were likely.

"Green up" referred to the spring when the grass poked up through the ground and turned green.

"Heel-fly time" occurred from mid-February to mid-April when the heel fly would sting the cattle in the tender part of their heels. In northern states, like Wyoming, heel-fly time is in midsummer.

"Turnout time" was in the spring when cattle were turned out to graze.

"Gathering time" occurred in the fall when cattle were selected for market. Cattle were often moved from summer pastures to wintering pastures nearer the ranch.

"Branding time" was late spring and into early summer.

Describe the Seasons

Come up with some of your own terms that describe the different activities that occur throughout the year where you live.

A Cowboy Takes Time for Some Shadin'

Shadin' was the term a cowboy used for resting. While riding the range on a hot summer day, a cowboy might stop at a shady spot and dismount. He would loosen the cinch on the saddle, allowing the horse's back to get some air. The cowboy would take the bit from the horse's mouth. Then he would hobble the horse, that is, tie a piece of leather around the horse's forefeet. The horse could graze, but not wander too far away. Then a cowboy might take off his hat and boots, rest in the shade, and dream of the future.

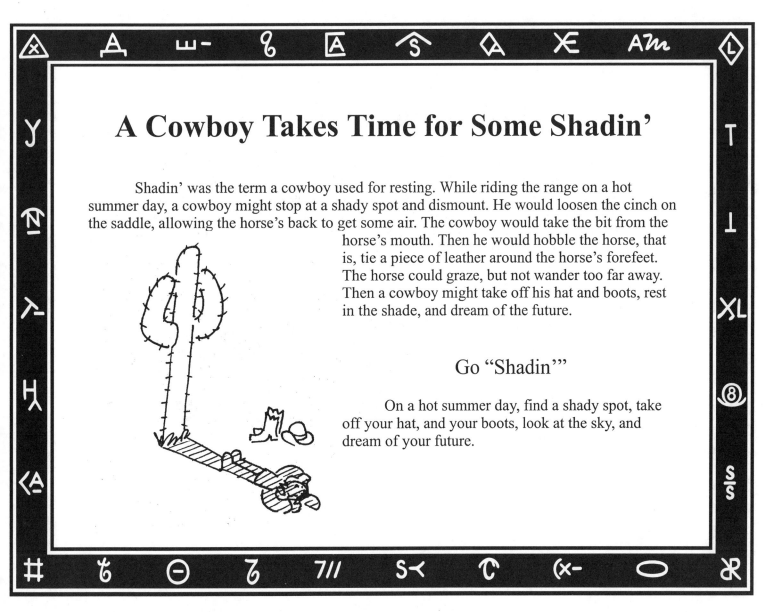

Go "Shadin'"

On a hot summer day, find a shady spot, take off your hat, and your boots, look at the sky, and dream of your future.

Cowboy Road Language

Most cowboys wave at others on country roads, whether they know the person or not. There's not much else to do and besides, it's a habit, and it's just plain common courtesy. Different waves can have different meanings. One finger in the air means, "Know you all my life." Two fingers raised from the steering wheel means, "Hello." And three fingers down and only the little finger in the air means, "Hi, I'm a dally roper." A dally roper turns his rope counterclockwise several times around the horn of the saddle when he's done throwing it.

Use Cowboy Road Language

Use some signs to put more meaning into your howdies. Some examples, could be, "Quick hello, but gotta go," or "Hi, gotta minute?"

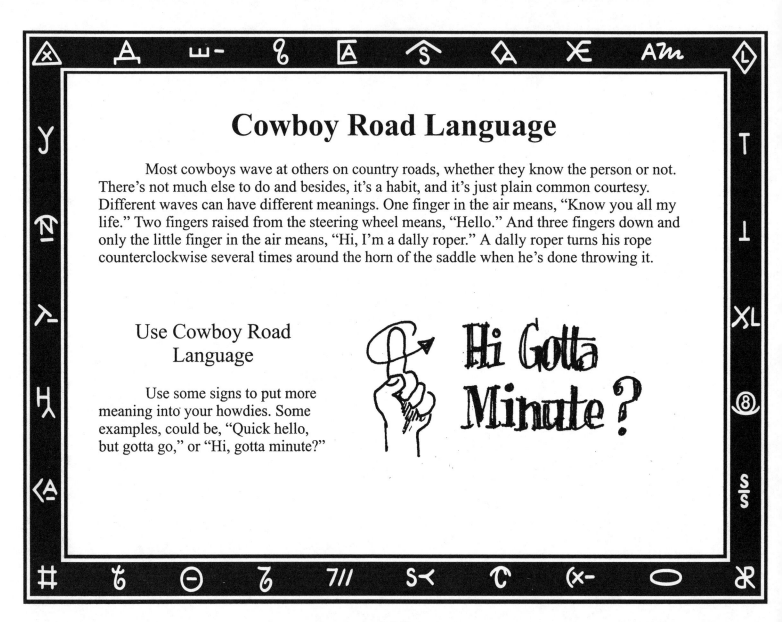

Cowboys Play Thimblerig

Thimblerig was a game played in the early West. It was later called the shell-game. The name "Thimblerig" came about because the game was originally played with three thimbles and a pea. The game can also be played with walnut shells, metal caps, or cups, and a small ball. In the game, the thimblerigger places a pea under one of three thimbles. Then he moves them around. The other player points to the thimble where he thinks the pea is hidden.

Play Thimblerig

Gather some friends. Find three cups and a small ball. Take turns being the thimblerigger who hides the ball under the cups and the players who guess where it's hidden.

Camp Cook Makes Substitutions

When supplies were scarce and ingredients lacking, the cooks made substitutions. They used experience and basic common sense to guide them. A camp cook didn't use written recipes. He could tell if a mixture was right by the look and feel of it. If the cook ran out of butter while cooking, he thinned some lard down with hot water and called it "Texas Butter." A similar substitution was called, "Prairie butter" it was the grease that was left from fried meat or bacon. Not only did the cook use "Prairie Butter" in recipes, cowboys spread it on bread and biscuits.

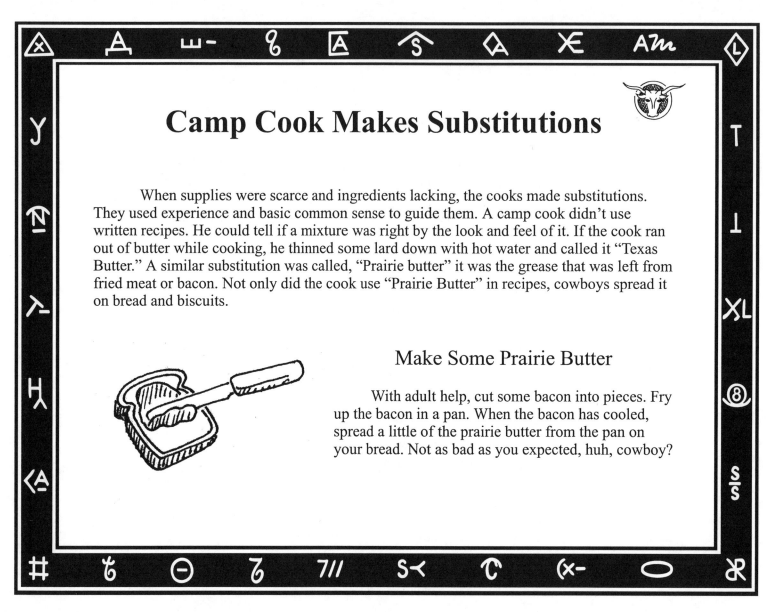

Make Some Prairie Butter

With adult help, cut some bacon into pieces. Fry up the bacon in a pan. When the bacon has cooled, spread a little of the prairie butter from the pan on your bread. Not as bad as you expected, huh, cowboy?

Cowboys Sent Signals

The cowboys of long ago used various methods to signal one another from a distance. To attract the attention of his pardner, the cowboy would swing his hat over his head from the right to the left. If he wanted to hurry up and talk to him, the cowboy rode his horse in small circles. When approaching someone he didn't know, a cowboy would raise his right arm to show he was a friend.

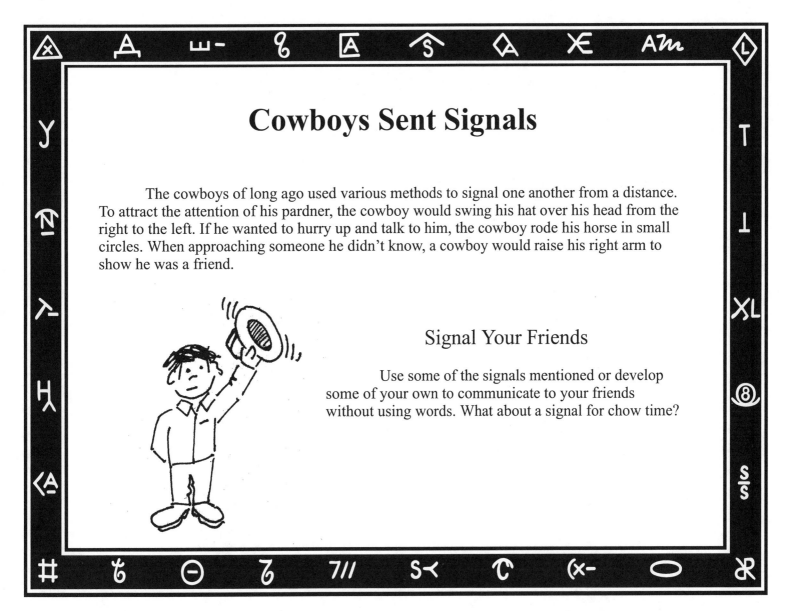

Signal Your Friends

Use some of the signals mentioned or develop some of your own to communicate to your friends without using words. What about a signal for chow time?

"Son-of-a-Gun" Stew

"Son-of-a-gun" stew was a famous dish of the cow camp cooks on the range. They didn't want to waste any meat, so they threw into a stew every part of a steer that could be swallowed, leaving out only the hoofs, hides, and horns. Cooks chopped up heart, tongue, liver, kidneys, sweetbreads, marrow gut, and tenderloin into small chunks. The pieces of meat were rolled in flour and browned in a Dutch oven. Fresh vegetables were usually not available, but sometimes potatoes, canned tomatoes, onions, and chiles were added for flavor. If you were a hungry cowboy after a hard days work, you'd eat about anything, including this stew. Make your own stew.

1 package chopped stew meat
1 package hearts and gizzards
2 cans beef broth
2 cans water
Small potatoes
1 can diced tomatoes
Salt
Pepper
Chiles (optional)

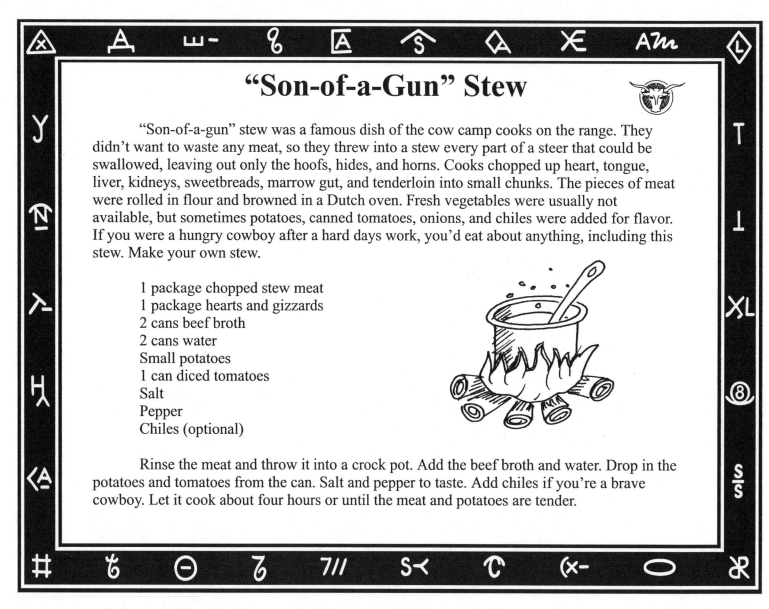

Rinse the meat and throw it into a crock pot. Add the beef broth and water. Drop in the potatoes and tomatoes from the can. Salt and pepper to taste. Add chiles if you're a brave cowboy. Let it cook about four hours or until the meat and potatoes are tender.

A Brand Book

A brand is a mark on the skin or hide of livestock or horses to show ownership of the animal. Ranchers used a variety of symbols, letters, and numbers. Brands were kept simple so they could be read from a distance. Many large ranches were known many miles away because of their brands. Some states and territories in the West developed brand books, which listed all the registered brands in the region. This brand book helped identify the owner of a stray.

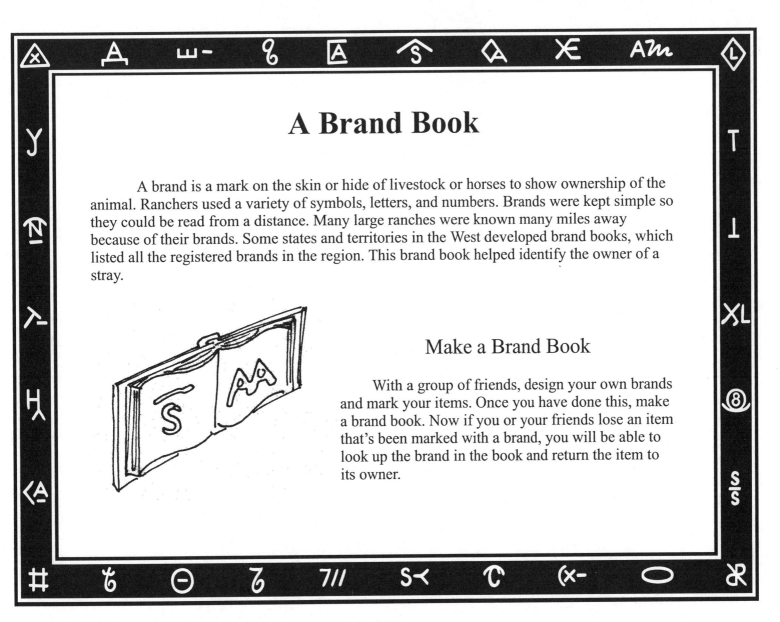

Make a Brand Book

With a group of friends, design your own brands and mark your items. Once you have done this, make a brand book. Now if you or your friends lose an item that's been marked with a brand, you will be able to look up the brand in the book and return the item to its owner.

Cowboy Lingo

Cowboys have their own lingo or slang. Much of their talk conjures up pictures in the mind. For example, here are several ways of saying I'm sick:

I have a headache built for a hoss.
I feel worse'n a calf with the slobbers.
I have to ride in the bed wagon.

Here are several ways you could tell a friend she is smart:

She is as sure as cockleburs on a coyote.
She is as smart as a bunkhouse rat.
She is like a prairie dog that knows her hole.

Talk Like a Cowboy

Come up with your own cowboy sayings about peace-making, snoring, bugs and varmints, bronc riding, or choose your own topic.

Cowboys Get a Pelon

The word pelon comes from the Mexican word *pilon* (pee-lo). It's a gratuity given by a seller to a buyer. In the West, a merchant gave a small gift, like candy, to a customer after he made a large purchase of supplies. The cowboys were always on the watch to see what pelon a merchant offered.

Give a Pelon to Your Customers

Have a pretend store. With some friends, gather items that ranchers would need to purchase, including small items to give as pelons. When customers make large purchases, give them a pelon to show your gratitude.

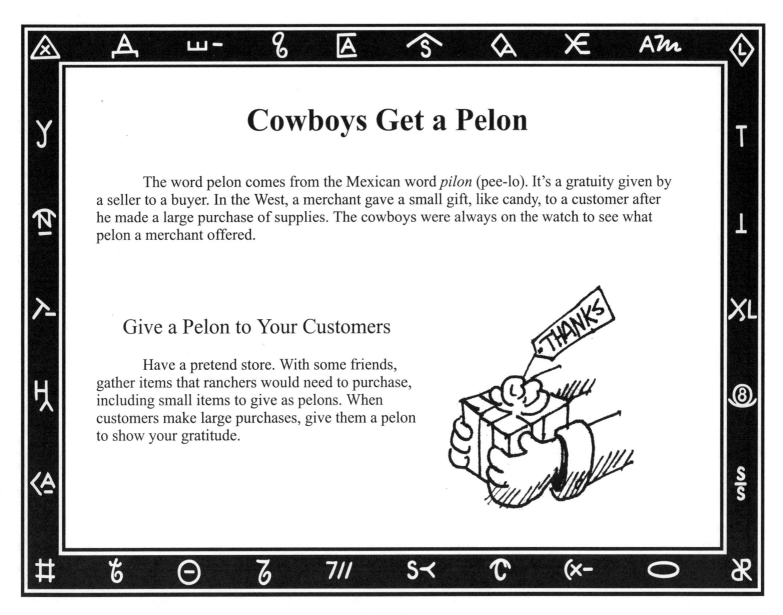

Eatin' Corn Pone

Corn pone is one name for cornmeal bread. Other names include Johnny cakes, corn dodgers and hush puppies. Texans rarely saw sourdough breads. It was more common on the High Plains, since dough spoiled in hot Texas weather. Besides, cornmeal was sometimes more plentiful than wheat flour. Here's a recipe:

2 cups corn meal
½ teaspoon salt
1 tablespoon margarine, lard, or bacon drippings
1 1/4 cups water

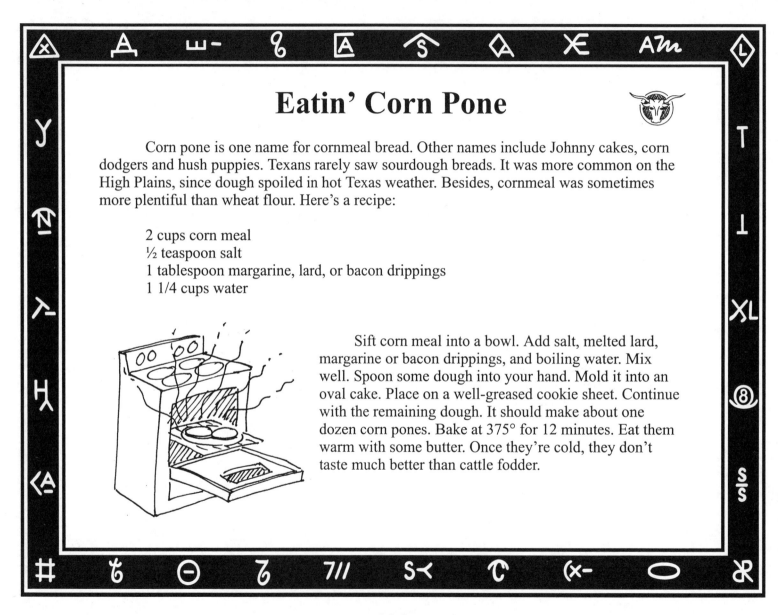

Sift corn meal into a bowl. Add salt, melted lard, margarine or bacon drippings, and boiling water. Mix well. Spoon some dough into your hand. Mold it into an oval cake. Place on a well-greased cookie sheet. Continue with the remaining dough. It should make about one dozen corn pones. Bake at 375° for 12 minutes. Eat them warm with some butter. Once they're cold, they don't taste much better than cattle fodder.

Cowboys Read the Stars

On the range, a cowboy slept out in the open under the bright stars. He could use the stars for information. On a clear night, he could watch the movement and position of the Big Dipper and roughly tell what time it was. The Big Dipper rotates around the North Star approximately once every 24 hours. Estimating time helped a cowboy know when his shift of riding herd was over. When stopping and setting up camp for the night, a cook might point the chuck wagon tongue toward the North Star. That's how he knew which direction to go the next morning.

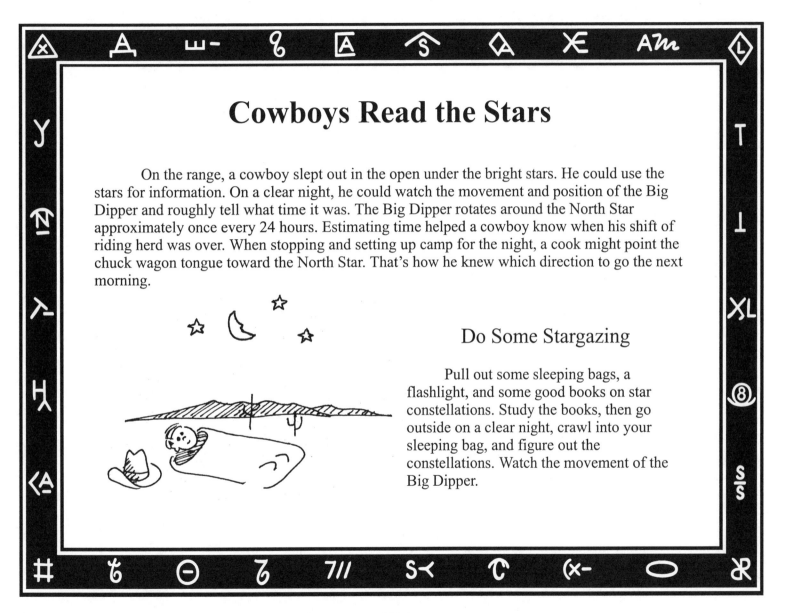

Do Some Stargazing

Pull out some sleeping bags, a flashlight, and some good books on star constellations. Study the books, then go outside on a clear night, crawl into your sleeping bag, and figure out the constellations. Watch the movement of the Big Dipper.

A Day in the Life of a Cowboy

Some of the phrases cowboys used came from experiences they had in their daily lives. After supper, one cowboy was heard saying, "That meat was so tough I even had to sharpen my knife to cut the gravy." Sounds like a cowboy that dug into some sorry grub. Another cowboy walked out of his bunkhouse and said, "That cowpuncher could talk the hide off a cow."

Make Up Some Cowboy Stories

Make up some stories using the above phrases. In the first scenario, you could make up a story about the camp cook that the cowboy had to ride trail with. How bad was the food? Did cowboys get sick? In the second scenario, you could write a story about a cowboy that talks too much. Does it get him into trouble? Does he drive the other cowboys loco? Have some fun with these, or make up some fun stories from some other phrases or scenarios.

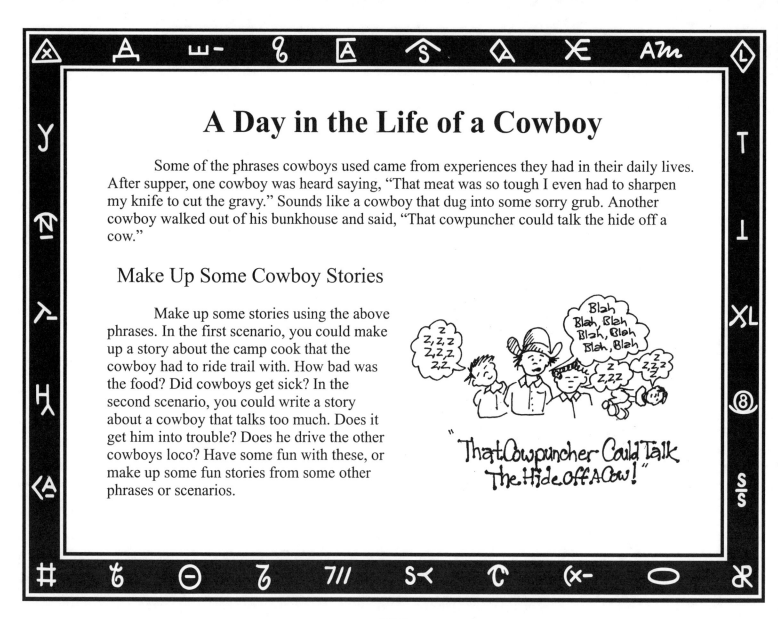

"That Cowpuncher Could Talk The Hide Off A Cow!"

122

Cowboys Wore Chaps

Cowboys wore chaps, (pronounced "shaps") to protect their legs. Chaps are seatless leather leggings, held up with a belt. Vaqueros, Mexican cowboys, wore them. The word originated from the Spanish word *chaparejos*. American cowboys discovered they protected them from prickly brush, rope burns, rain and snow, horse bites, and other ranch hazards. There are several different styles of chaps. In earlier times, cowboys wore chaps called shotguns. They climbed into these tube-like leggings. "Batwings" are chaps with extra wide flaps. They wrapped around and fastened behind the legs. "Woollies" are made of sheepskin and are worn with the wool or hair on the outside. Cowboys on the northern plains wore them for warmth.

Make Some Chaps

Get permission from your trail boss or a parent to cut an old pair of oversized pants into chaps. Begin at the bottom and cut along the outer seam on one side of the pants. At the top, cut off the back of the pants along the waistband and keep cutting down the opposite pant seam. Begin at the bottom again and cut up the inseam and back down the other side. Now pull the chaps over your pants before you go searching for cattle among the bushes and brush.

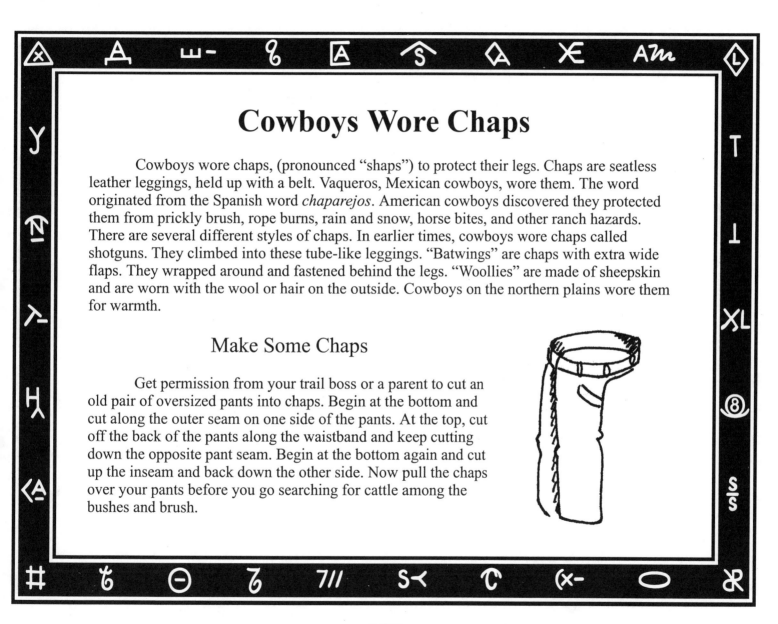

Warm Biscuits, Yum!

Cowboys liked their bread warm at every meal. Serving cold bread was an insult. Fresh warm bread was not always available, but most cooks could turn out warm biscuits. Some cowboys had different names for sourdough biscuits, such as "dough gods," "pancake splatters," or "saddle blankets." To make the sourdough starter you will need:

2 cups unsifted flour
2 tablespoons sugar
1 ½ tablespoons salt
1 ½ cups water
1 tablespoon vinegar

To make the starter, combine the flour, sugar and salt. Pour in the water and vinegar. Stir well. Cover with a cloth and keep in a warm place. When it smells mighty sour, it's ready to use. To make the biscuits you will need:

1 ½ cups flour
1/4 teaspoon baking soda
½ teaspoon salt
2 teaspoons baking powder
1/4 cup melted butter or margarine

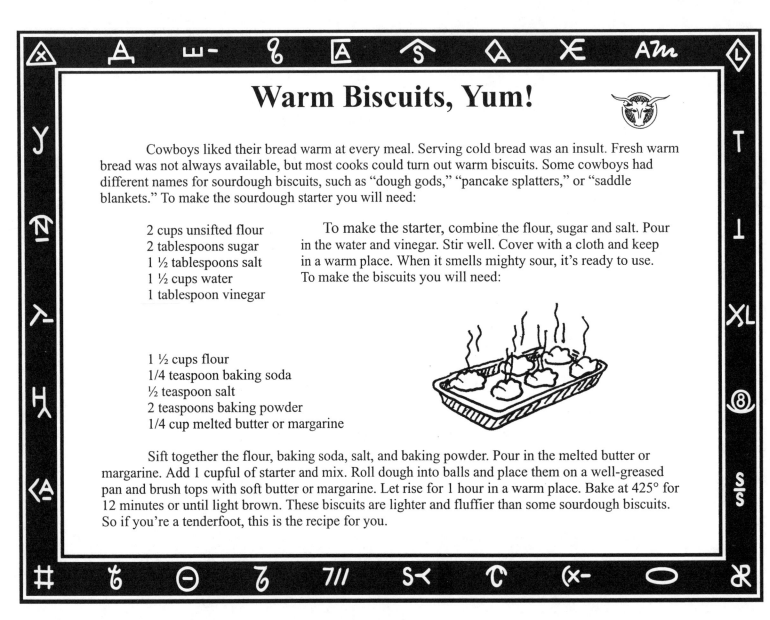

Sift together the flour, baking soda, salt, and baking powder. Pour in the melted butter or margarine. Add 1 cupful of starter and mix. Roll dough into balls and place them on a well-greased pan and brush tops with soft butter or margarine. Let rise for 1 hour in a warm place. Bake at 425° for 12 minutes or until light brown. These biscuits are lighter and fluffier than some sourdough biscuits. So if you're a tenderfoot, this is the recipe for you.

A Trail Count

A trail count was a method of counting cattle as they were strung along on a trail drive. Once the cattle left the ranch, the trail boss chose one man to be stationed on the opposite side of the trail from him. They each took a separate count of the cattle as they passed, pointing to each animal, as they counted it. When they reached one hundred, they dropped a pebble into a pocket or tied a knot in a string. When the cattle had all passed by, the cowboys totaled their counts. Most of the time their counts came out the same, but if there was a big discrepancy, they rode to the beginning of the herd and started over again.

Take a Trail Count

When you are out on a trail ride to the grocery store to get some grub, count the cars you pass. Mark each ten by putting a slash on a piece of paper or like the cowboys did, put a rock in your pocket. Take a friend along and compare your totals at the end.

A Cowboy's Poncho

A poncho is a blanket-like covering with a hole in the center for the head to fit through. The poncho sits on the shoulders of a cowboy and helps keep him dry on rainy days. *Vaqueros*, Mexican cowboys, wore a similar covering made of wool, called a *serape*.

Make a Poncho

Ask your rancher or parent for an old shower curtain, tarp, sheet, or blanket. Spread your tarp on the floor. Now fold it in half. Lie with arms along the fold. You want the poncho to reach your wrists. Have a friend trim off the excess material on the sides and along the bottom. The tarp should hang to about knee length. Cut a hole in the center of the tarp large enough for your head to fit through. Now wear your poncho on those rainy days when you're out working in the yard. Oops, I mean "on the range."

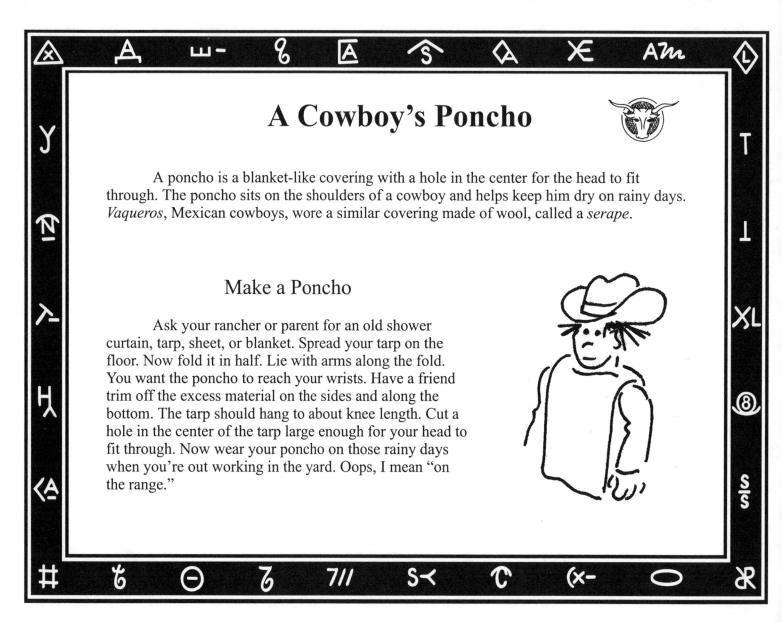

Roping is a Skill

Cattle had to be roped to be branded, medicated, and sometimes moved to another pasture. Roping them was one of the hardest skills a cowboy had to master. He had to become a good judge of distance, speed, and have split-second timing to catch them. It took years of experience to predict what the animals might do.

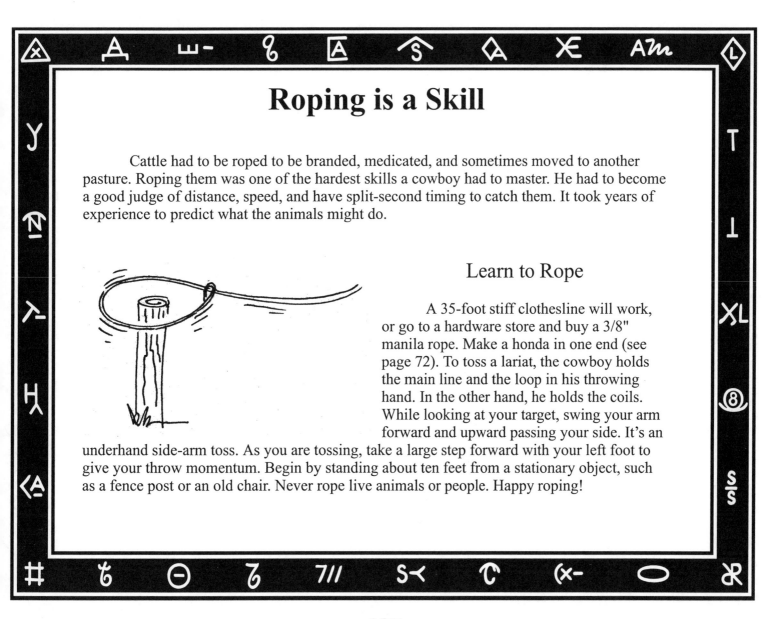

Learn to Rope

A 35-foot stiff clothesline will work, or go to a hardware store and buy a 3/8" manila rope. Make a honda in one end (see page 72). To toss a lariat, the cowboy holds the main line and the loop in his throwing hand. In the other hand, he holds the coils. While looking at your target, swing your arm forward and upward passing your side. It's an underhand side-arm toss. As you are tossing, take a large step forward with your left foot to give your throw momentum. Begin by standing about ten feet from a stationary object, such as a fence post or an old chair. Never rope live animals or people. Happy roping!

Saddle Blankets

A cowboy placed a blanket under a saddle to protect his horse from getting saddle sores. Some of the blankets used in the old days were woven by the Navajo Indians. The background colors on these blankets were usually white or gray with red and black triangle and diamond patterns. The blankets measured approximately 2 ½ feet square.

Make a Saddle Blanket

Find some material with a light colored background, like white, light gray, or tan. Cut it to size. Cut some sponges into shapes, such as triangles and diamonds. Dip them into tempera paint and stamp the shapes onto your material. When the material is dry, it is ready to throw onto the back of your horse. Once the saddle is on and before you cinch it up, stick a couple of fingers under the blanket where it comes over the withers. This gives it a little slack. If you don't have a horse, use your saddle blanket to decorate your bunkhouse.

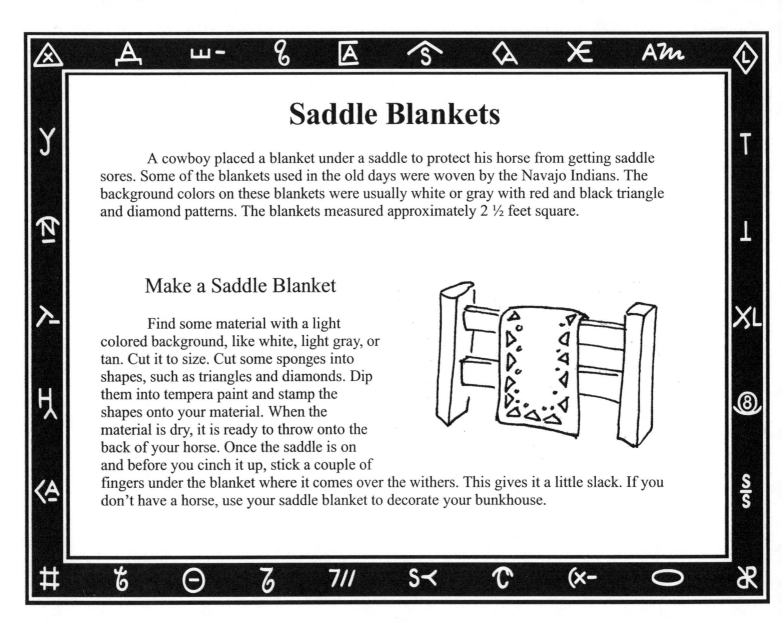

Hard-Working Cowboys

A cowboy was a laborer hired to tend cattle. He had many duties that took him into all kinds of terrain. A cowboy had to ride fences, round up cattle, and drive cattle along trails. Cowboying was a strenuous, dirty job with long hours and for minimal pay. A cowboy wasn't much for complaining either. Instead, the dangers and difficulties he had to overcome were a source of pride for him.

Create a Cowboy Obstacle Course

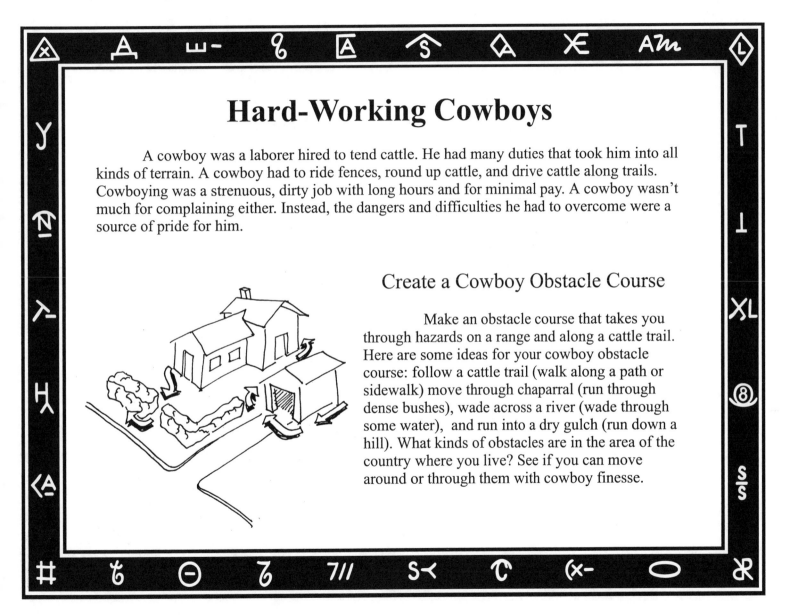

Make an obstacle course that takes you through hazards on a range and along a cattle trail. Here are some ideas for your cowboy obstacle course: follow a cattle trail (walk along a path or sidewalk) move through chaparral (run through dense bushes), wade across a river (wade through some water), and run into a dry gulch (run down a hill). What kinds of obstacles are in the area of the country where you live? See if you can move around or through them with cowboy finesse.

Cowboys Liked Music

Not only did cowboys sing, they played musical instruments too. While some instruments, like a guitar, were too big and bulky to take on a cattle drive, they could take harmonicas, and occasionally a fiddle made it into the chuck wagon. If they didn't have instruments, they clapped their hands. Cowboys used the music to entertain themselves and to calm the cattle.

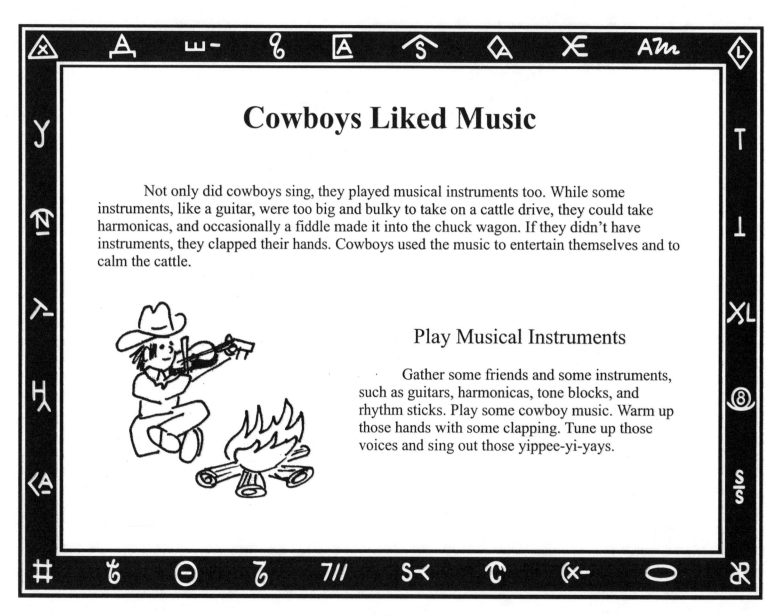

Play Musical Instruments

Gather some friends and some instruments, such as guitars, harmonicas, tone blocks, and rhythm sticks. Play some cowboy music. Warm up those hands with some clapping. Tune up those voices and sing out those yippee-yi-yays.

Rope-Making

Some of the ropes cowboys used were made from hemp. This fiber makes a good all-around rope. In making these ropes, fibers are twisted together similar to a piece of yarn. Then the yarn is formed into strands. The final step in the process is called "laying the rope." Three strands are laid beside one another and twisted in the opposite direction of the twist in the strands.

Make a Rope

To make a rope, cut four pieces of yarn the same length. Fold your strands of yarn in half. Put a pencil through the fold and find a friend to hold that end. You hold onto the opposite end. Facing each other, stretch the yarn between you. Wind the yarn, turning in one direction, while your friend turns it in the opposite direction. Once taut, remove the pencil, but continue to have your friend hold his end. Fold the yarn in half, by taking your end over to the end your friend is holding. Your friend holds the two ends together while you grasp the middle of the yarn. Now loosen your grip. The four strands will start to twist together to make a rope.

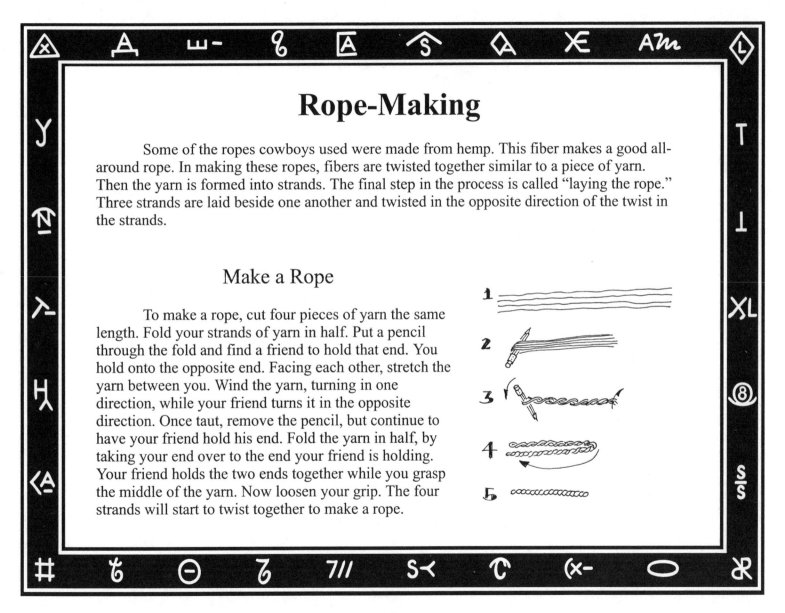

The Cowboy's Saddle

A cowboy didn't necessarily own his horse, but he usually owned his saddle. He sat on it most of the day and part of the night, so he was very fussy about it. A cowboy would give a month's pay for a carefully crafted saddle. It could last him a good 30 years. A comfortable saddle wasn't important just to the cowboy, but to the horse too. A poorly made saddle could rub blisters on a horse's back. If a cowboy needed money, he would sell everything but his saddle. Without a saddle, he couldn't find work as a cowboy. The saddle was not only practical, but sometimes it was a "work of art," ornamented with a flash of silver and decorative stamping. To stamp a saddle, the saddle maker first dampened the leather, then pounded and gouged his patterns into it. He used stains, oils, and varnishes to give his designs more character.

Stamp a Pattern on Your Saddle

To make a saddle, find a large piece of corrugated cardboard. Dampen it. Using some instruments, such as forks, keys, pencils, pens, toothpicks, and paper clips, etch a pattern in the cardboard. Once it has dried, take colored pencils and add some color and definition to the patterns you created. Stand back to see your final work of art. Now throw it on your hoss and ride into the sunset.

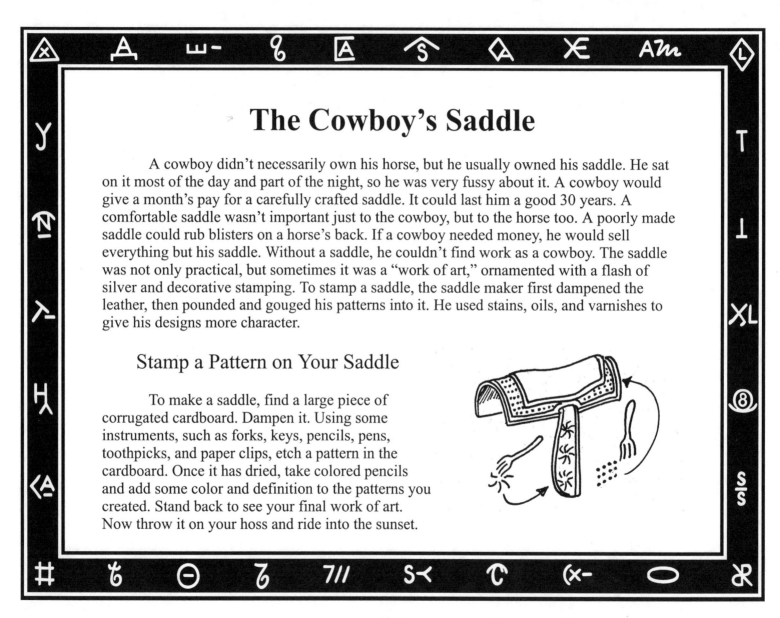

Prairie Pillows

A cowboy's bedroll was stored in the chuck wagon, where there wasn't room for extra things. A cowboy didn't have a soft fluffy pillow. He slept on blankets on the ground. He rolled a shirt or extra pair of pants and tucked it under his head for the night. This bedroll became his bed. In the morning, the cowboy was responsible for making his bed, that is, rolling up his bedding and storing it in or near the chuck wagon. If he didn't get it loaded, the camp cook might just leave it behind.

Make a Prairie Pillow

To make a prairie pillow, stuff some clean clothing into a pillowcase. Tie it closed with a piece of string. Now take a rest using your prairie pillow. A might lumpy, but better'n nothin'.

The Pony Express Routes

The Pony Express routes wound over mountains and across plains and desert lands. In addition to the rough terrain, the Pony Express riders and their horses sometimes encountered bad weather. They faced flooded rivers, where horses were swept away. In winter, snowstorms hid the trail. At times they had to lead their horses over the mountains. Wind blew dust in their faces, and rains pelted them.

Set Up a Pony Express Route

Set up your own course winding your trail through rocks and hills you have in your area. Add some other elements, by turning on the sprinkler, filling a small swimming pool with water, and filling a tub with mud. Find some flat open boxes, like the kind that soda cans come in. Fill the boxes with various items, such as ice cubes, sand, and rocks. Now run through your own Pony Express route.

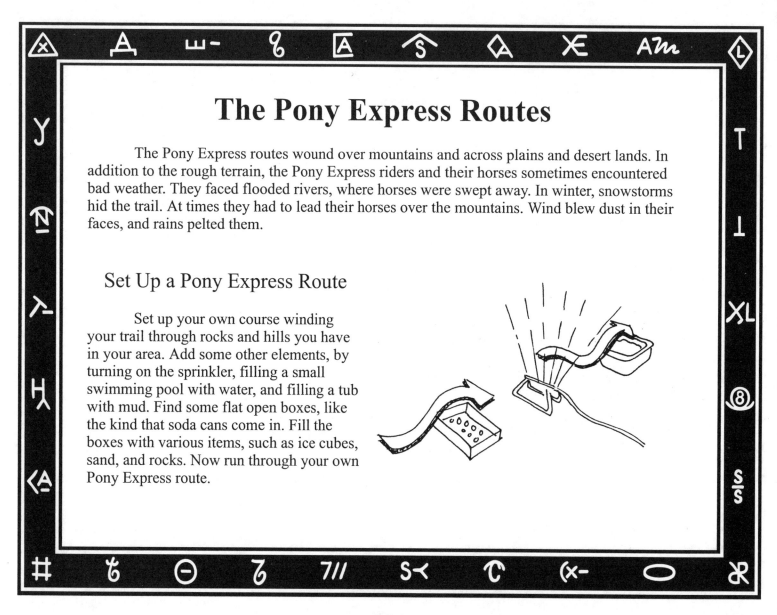

A Cowboy's Rope Has to Feel Right

A cowboy didn't want a rope that was too stiff. Instead, he wanted it to feel just right. But atmospheric conditions could take a rope in top condition and ruin it. For example, a rope exposed to salty air along the coast would harden. When a cowboy traveled in this part of the country, he stored his rope in a can to protect it.

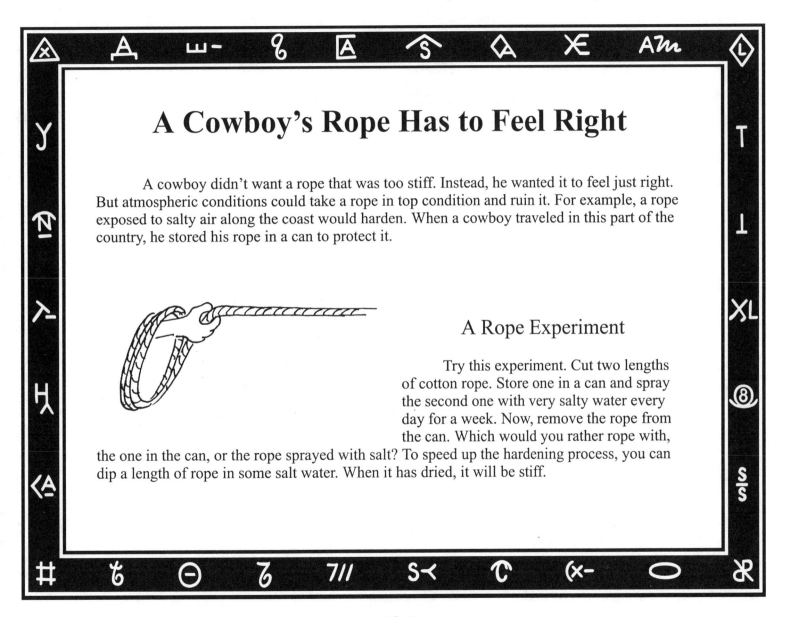

A Rope Experiment

Try this experiment. Cut two lengths of cotton rope. Store one in a can and spray the second one with very salty water every day for a week. Now, remove the rope from the can. Which would you rather rope with, the one in the can, or the rope sprayed with salt? To speed up the hardening process, you can dip a length of rope in some salt water. When it has dried, it will be stiff.

A Cowboy's Pants

Take the "distressed" blue jean test. A lot can be said about how hard a cowboy works by looking at the wear and tear of his jeans. Take the test below. Give one point to each of the ten items listed that fits your most worn-out pair of blue jeans.

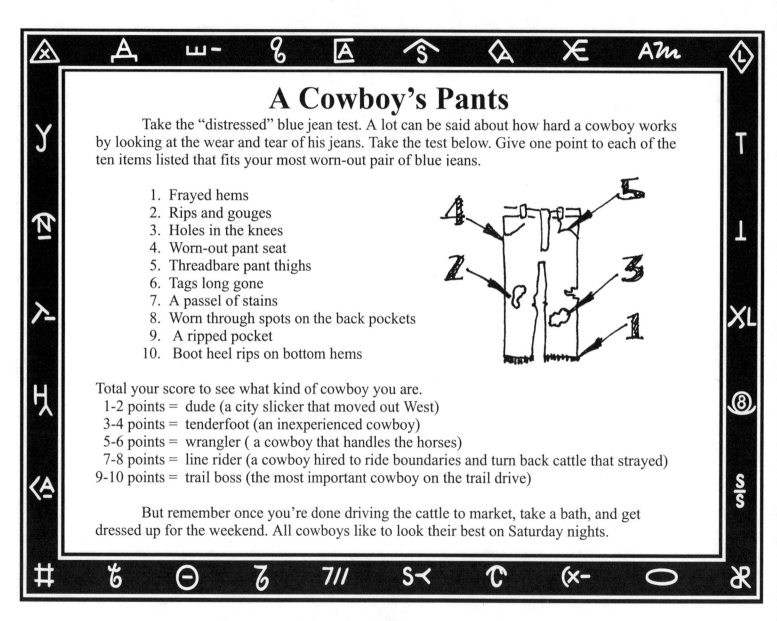

1. Frayed hems
2. Rips and gouges
3. Holes in the knees
4. Worn-out pant seat
5. Threadbare pant thighs
6. Tags long gone
7. A passel of stains
8. Worn through spots on the back pockets
9. A ripped pocket
10. Boot heel rips on bottom hems

Total your score to see what kind of cowboy you are.
  1-2 points = dude (a city slicker that moved out West)
  3-4 points = tenderfoot (an inexperienced cowboy)
  5-6 points = wrangler (a cowboy that handles the horses)
  7-8 points = line rider (a cowboy hired to ride boundaries and turn back cattle that strayed)
9-10 points = trail boss (the most important cowboy on the trail drive)

But remember once you're done driving the cattle to market, take a bath, and get dressed up for the weekend. All cowboys like to look their best on Saturday nights.

A Cowboy Souvenir Photo

Many young men wanted adventure and followed their dreams of heading west to become cowboys. These cowpokes helped drive cattle to markets in railroad cow towns. At the end of the trail, the first thing the cowboys did, was hoof it to the nearest hotel for baths. After all, they'd been living in the same soiled clothes for the last several months. Once cleaned up, they headed for the barber for a shave and a haircut. Dressed in their best clothing, they hiked to the photographer's studio. The cowboys wanted to send souvenir photos of themselves to their kinfolk back home.

Take Some Souvenir Cowboy Photos

Get permission from your rancher to use a camera. Now find a friend. Dressed in your best cowboy attire, take turns taking photos. Send them to your family and friends, showing them you participated in all the activities in this book. Congratulations! You are a full fledged cowboy or cowgirl. Whoopee!

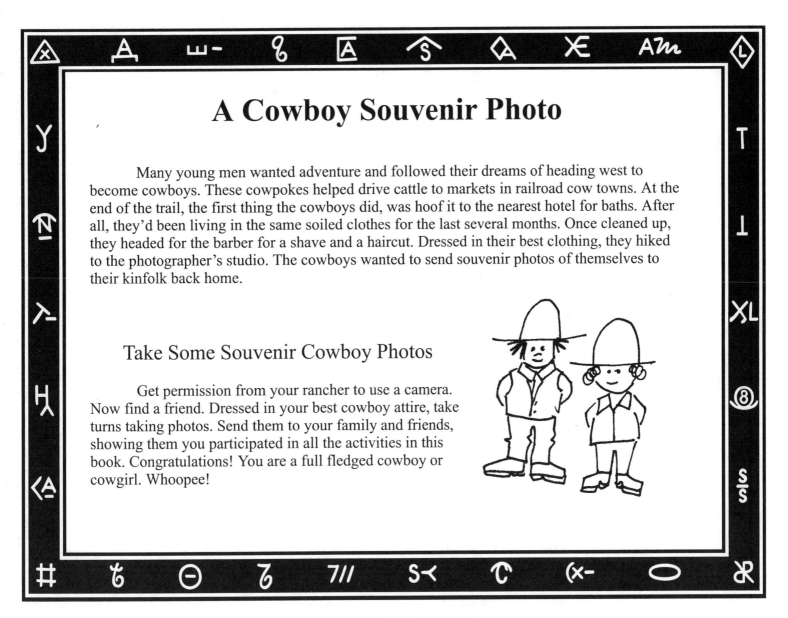

Cowboy Weathermen

It's not surprising that cowboys talked a lot about the weather, because it had a big influence on their work. All cattlemen liked rain because it made the grass grow. Plentiful grass created fatter steers. But too much rain could cause problems. On a trail drive, cattle could be swept downstream on swollen rivers or they could get bogged in quicksand and have to be pulled free. Cowboys have seen droughts, when the rivers dry up and grasslands turn into deserts.

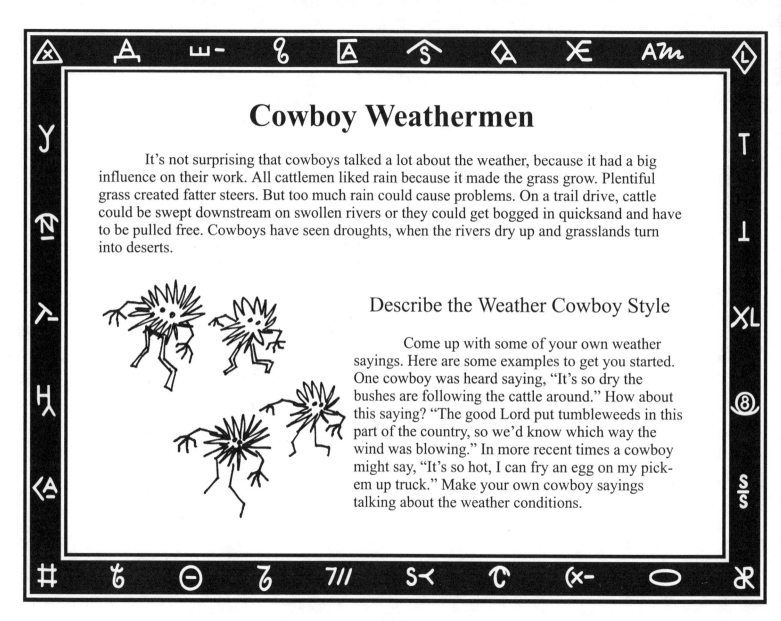

Describe the Weather Cowboy Style

Come up with some of your own weather sayings. Here are some examples to get you started. One cowboy was heard saying, "It's so dry the bushes are following the cattle around." How about this saying? "The good Lord put tumbleweeds in this part of the country, so we'd know which way the wind was blowing." In more recent times a cowboy might say, "It's so hot, I can fry an egg on my pick-em up truck." Make your own cowboy sayings talking about the weather conditions.

A Cowboy's Living Quarters

After the fall roundup, a rancher didn't need as many ranch hands. During the winter, he kept only a few cowboys. These ranch hands were willing to work for a roof over their heads and some chow. They lived in a bunkhouse, which was a crude shack made from logs or weatherboard. About ten cowboys shared a bunkhouse. It became a rather messy, smelly place. Sometimes cowboys painted their shacks with whitewash or papered them with magazines and mail-order catalogs. This gave them something to read when they were bored and helped somewhat to protect against the cold winter drafts.

Make a Bunkhouse

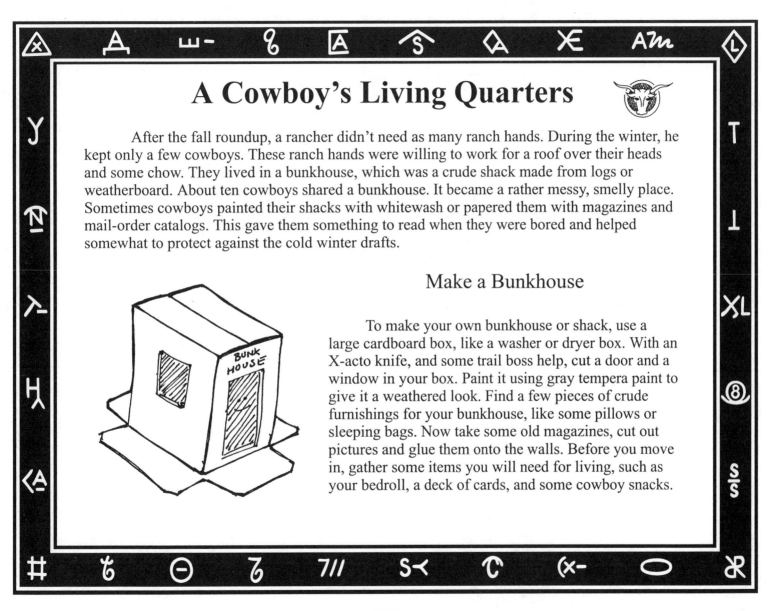

To make your own bunkhouse or shack, use a large cardboard box, like a washer or dryer box. With an X-acto knife, and some trail boss help, cut a door and a window in your box. Paint it using gray tempera paint to give it a weathered look. Find a few pieces of crude furnishings for your bunkhouse, like some pillows or sleeping bags. Now take some old magazines, cut out pictures and glue them onto the walls. Before you move in, gather some items you will need for living, such as your bedroll, a deck of cards, and some cowboy snacks.

Havin' A Hoedown

A hoedown is the cowboy's name for a lively, rollicking dance. Cowboys worked hard most of the time, so they looked forward to special events, such as the occasional dance. They cleaned up, slicked down their hair, shined up their boots and spurs, and put on their best clothes. Most of the time there weren't many females, so some cowboys put on aprons or tied handkerchiefs around their sleeves and danced the part of the women.

Have a hoedown with some friends. Put on your Sunday best cowboy duds. Play some square dance or country western tunes. Clap your hands and stomp your feet. Put the ladies in the center of a circle and the guys around the outside. Grab a partner and shuffle those boots. Pick someone to be the caller and call out the words and steps of a square dance. A caller makes up words as he goes, to fit the occasion. Here's two verses of a dance to get you started:

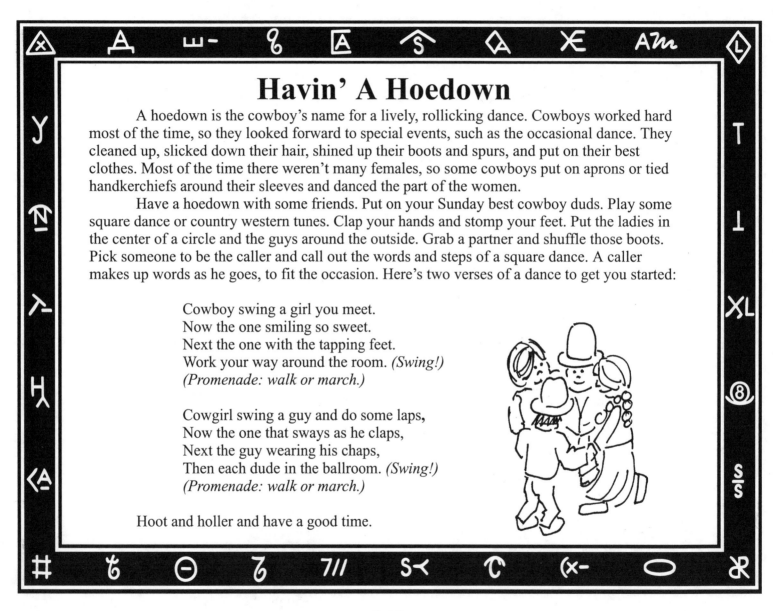

Cowboy swing a girl you meet.
Now the one smiling so sweet.
Next the one with the tapping feet.
Work your way around the room. *(Swing!)*
(Promenade: walk or march.)

Cowgirl swing a guy and do some laps,
Now the one that sways as he claps,
Next the guy wearing his chaps,
Then each dude in the ballroom. *(Swing!)*
(Promenade: walk or march.)

Hoot and holler and have a good time.

The Demand for Cowboys Changes

The era of the cowboy reached its peak with the boom in beef, around 1882 and 1883. But the boom was about to come to an end. The Homestead Act passed by Congress made land available to settlers. Homesteaders started moving west and claiming land for farming. Land where cattle once grazed and roamed free, became fenced in. Cattle ranchers soon followed suit and fenced in their land holdings. Railroads extended farther west and south, which meant cowboys no longer needed to drive cattle to northern railroads.

While the weather had been moderate most winters, that changed in the winter of '85-'86. Thousands of cattle froze in bitter cold weather. The following summer, when a drought dried up springs and watering holes, many cattle died from lack of water. The following winter, was brutal as well, with the heaviest snowfall and blizzard conditions that the ranchers had yet to experience. In earlier times, cattle moved ahead of snowstorms, but now they were stopped in their tracks by fencing. Large herds of cattle froze.

Along with bad weather and fencing, there was more beef available than buyers for it, so beef prices dropped. The way ranches were run changed. They became more self-sufficient, growing their own hay. The great beef bonanza had come to an end. The twenty-year era of the cattle boom was over.

About the Author and Illustrator

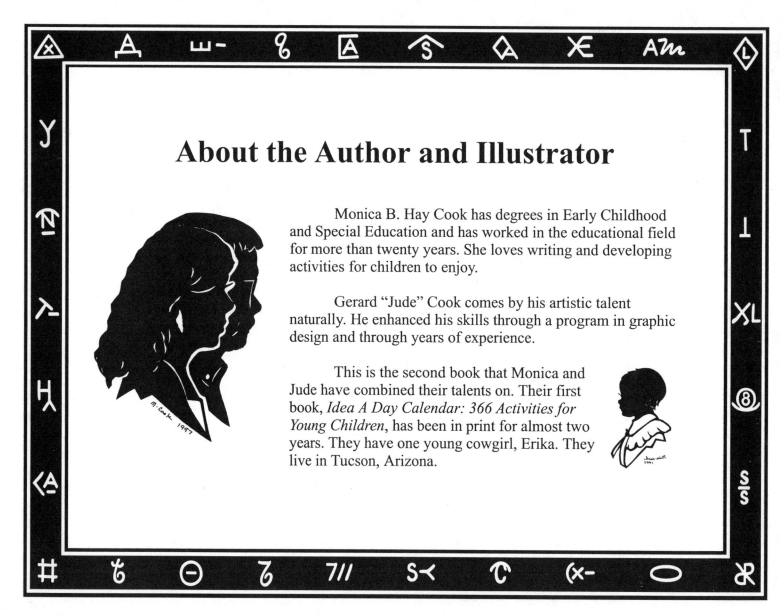

Monica B. Hay Cook has degrees in Early Childhood and Special Education and has worked in the educational field for more than twenty years. She loves writing and developing activities for children to enjoy.

Gerard "Jude" Cook comes by his artistic talent naturally. He enhanced his skills through a program in graphic design and through years of experience.

This is the second book that Monica and Jude have combined their talents on. Their first book, *Idea A Day Calendar: 366 Activities for Young Children*, has been in print for almost two years. They have one young cowgirl, Erika. They live in Tucson, Arizona.

Ordering Information

Name_____

Address_____

City_____ State_____ Zip_____

E-mail address_____

Would you like the book(s) autographed?_____

If so, to whom?_____

_____Copies of **Kickin' Up Some Cowboy Fun** @ $14.95 $_____

U.S. Postage & Handling: $4.00 each $_____

Additional Copies (U.S.) Postage & Handling $2.00 each $_____

International Postage & Handling: $9.00 each $_____

Additional copies (International) Postage & Handling $5.00 $_____

Total amount enclosed $_____

Please send check or money order to:

Monjeu Press
P.O. Box 64353
Tucson, Az 85728-4353
Phone (520) 293-4908
Fax (520) 622-2959